A true novel of strength and encouragement.

Those
HOLLAND KIDS

then and now

A memoir from letters of love and laughter written to last a lifetime.

Donna Holland Lawrence

Those Holland Kids
Copyright © 2011 Donna Holland Lawrence

All Rights Reserved.

No part of this publication may be reproduced, stored in a retrieval system, or transmitted in any form or by any means – electronic, mechanical, photocopying, recording, or otherwise - without the written permission of the author or publisher. The only exception is brief quotations in printed reviews.

First published by Holland Publishing House
ISBN 978-0-9846507-5-0

Printed in the United States of America.

This book is printed on acid-free paper.

HOLLAND PUBLISHING HOUSE
P.O. Box 785
Stone Mountain, GA 30086

DEDICATION

This book is dedicated to the memory of my mother and my father, the parents of those Holland kids. Kenneth Holland was a man of many talents, and lover of knowledge and music. His desire was to pass them on to his children. Idona Holland was a lover of her family and her God. Her desire was for the two to become acquainted and deeply bonded.

The book is also dedicated to one of those Holland kids, my sister, Cecelia (Jenny), who kept excitement and laughter in the family from childhood on into her adult life. Although she is greatly missed, her absence does not make a break in the Holland chain. She is kept alive in our hearts and in things such as this book.

ACKNOWLEDGEMENTS

First of all, I give all of the credit to my Lord and Saviour, Jesus Christ. He, alone, made it possible.

Second, Barbara Holland Coleman, Charlotte Holland Gaines and Jessie Holland Howard, my dear sisters and friends worked tirelessly. They supplied me with information and insight. They gave speedy responses to my many requests for more information and detail. Without their love and their amazing recall and articulation of events, this book would not have been possible.

A special thanks to my granddaughter, Dey Lynn Morris, for giving her computer technical expertise, her time and talent creating and drawing the precious picture used at the end of the book.

Prologue

It's a cold wintry weekend at the Holland family home in 1951. As usual in Indiana, freshly fallen snow lies in drifts along the walkway and against the gray wood frame of the small two-story dwelling. The Holland house is the smallest of the eighteen to twenty that line either side of the 500 block of Brackenridge Street. The number 526 above the door glitters in the rays of sunshine that seem purposefully directed through the frigid atmosphere down upon the tiny structure.

Inside, the rustle of quiet, early morning chatter and lazy weekend activity is interrupted by the seemingly too-shrill ring of the telephone. "Who could be calling at this hour?" Mother, Idona, mutters as she reaches for the phone, and her household of nine children gathers around. There has been a fatal accident at the facility where Daddy is hospitalized. After such a long absence from the family, the sudden realization that he will not be coming home turns the tranquil mood of the day to one of varying depths of astonishment and disbelief.

Idona and her seven daughters seek comfort, as they often did, huddling around the old coal-burning stove, their only source of heat for the entire house. Her two young sons have retreated to their room upstairs. Outside the familiar Indiana March winds whistle. The gloom inside causes little minds to wonder about the future. They know now that Daddy is gone forever. Both good and bad memories linger.

Because Idona loved him dearly, she endured his many weaknesses that somehow did not outweigh his many attributes. Everyone who knew her credited her strength as a survivor to her relationship with Jehovah Elohim who created her as a humble, quiet-spirited woman of God. She trusted Him as her Jehovah El Elyon, the Sovereign Ruler not only of the universe but also of her family. It was these strengths and attributes that encouraged the hearts of her children to write the pages that follow.

Who actually are "Those Holland Kids?" A family that remained close while growing up in Fort Wayne, a small town in Indiana. As adults they became separated by geographical distance, but came up with a way to stay intimately connected. Idona's seven daughters began a lively correspondence in the form of quarterly newsletters. Those colorful pages of orange, blue, green, purple or yellow became popular not only to extended family members, but also to friends and neighbors.

In a world where the numbers of close-knit families seem to be dwindling astronomically this example of chitchatting and jovial nostalgia has served as a source of comfort and intrigue to many people. The grace and favor of Almighty God has shown so much upon these letters, letters that have travelled across many miles year after year. This captivating story from the correspondence of six surviving sisters depicts how God can and does work to restore and maintain the unity of the family.

May God's Grace and Mercy be upon you, the reader, and your family!

CONTENTS

Chapter 1 - One Glorious Reunion 1

Chapter 2 - Distressing Realities of the Past 21

Chapter 3 - A Dream Come True; The First Family Newsletter 33

Chapter 4 - Looking Back/Getting Reacquainted 47

Chapter 5 - What! An Early End to Our Newsletter? 63

Chapter 6 - Remembering Mama 79

Chapter 7 - The Thief Cometh to Kill, Steal and Destroy 93

Chapter 8 - Struggles For Health/The Battle Begins 107

Chapter 9 - Losing the Battle/Winning the War 125

Chapter 10 - Remembering Jenny 137

Chapter 11 - Loads of Laughter/Extractions From Many Letters 147

Chapter 12 - Those Holland Kids, "NOW" 201

Epilogue 209

chapter 1

October 1995
One glorious reunion

Accompanied by four of her sisters, Cecelia confidently steers her brand-new maroon-colored Mercury van as it speeds along Highway 175 South toward Atlanta. She sighs in relief, squinting at the surprisingly vivid road sign. "Thirty-eight miles to Atlanta and I've driven almost all the way by myself with energy to spare." Cecelia, always known as Jenny, is the fourth of the nine Holland siblings.

Barbara, called Bibba or Barb, seated directly behind Cecelia, seems almost too relaxed since her open book is about to slide from her lap. She is intrigued by Jenny's performance at the wheel after so many gruesome hours on the road. Her mind begins slipping backward in time. "How clearly I remember when Jenny was two or three years old," she muses. "She would often run outside with only her birthday suit on and her hair standing up all over her head. Because she had beautiful, long, black, naturally curly hair, her second nickname was Little Gypsy. She was a mischievous child but also very loving, always hugging on Mom. For some reason she loved attempting to comb her sisters' hair even though she was usually at odds with us. Jenny had a terrible temper and displayed it by chasing us through the house with a butcher knife in her hands. Now that I think about it, I wonder what she would have done if she had caught any of us!

"When we were at play, Jenny evidently felt she owned the ball because when she became upset with us she would take the ball and leave. As I look back, I really don't think any of us were jealous of her very fair complexion and beautiful hair; at least I know I wasn't. I was like a second mother to her since I had to help raise her and the others under her. I don't believe she was even conscious that she was different from the rest of us. It was probably her mischievous spirit that caused us to exclude her from our activities at times. I feel pangs of remorse as I reflect on those and many other thoughtless childhood situations.

"During Cecelia's teen years her fun-loving nature made her somewhat wild. I still have a picture of her dancing with someone, a cigarette hanging out of her mouth. She could easily appear tough and harsh, but Cecelia actually had a very tender heart and was never mean to anyone. I believe all she wanted was some attention. Now that she's settled down, she is a good wife and mother of six, an immaculate housekeeper, and the best cook of all us sisters. I'm happy that we're neighbors and in the same subdivision.

Those Holland Kids

I have become accustomed to her calling every morning with the familiar question, 'Whatcha doin' today?' How I enjoy our trips to the health food store and her teaching me about organic foods."

Barbara begins to smile at her thoughts. "Jenny has such a sense of humor she could easily have been a standup comedian. Oh, how she cracks jokes about all of us, especially me. I don't take her seriously because I know she is just being witty, just being herself. She is always the life of the party."

Barbara is suddenly jolted into the present by Cecelia's burst of laughter. Charlotte, or Sharkie to her sisters, seated in the front passenger seat, tickles Jenny's funny bone as she chatters excitedly about some incident on her job. Charlotte's work experiences are always worthy of popcorn and soda pop. "Hmmm, I guess I must have missed this latest happening by daydreaming," Barbara concludes. She becomes concerned about where her reading glasses might be. She glances around for them briefly but her attention has been diverted to the front passenger seat.

"Charlotte, being the third child in our family," she reminisces, "always causes me to remember two basic things about her childhood. When she was two or three years old Mom and Dad had filled an old washtub with water so we could dunk for apples at Halloween. I owned a toy clicker bug and was scaring Charlotte with it. Backing away from me, she fell into the tub of water and nearly drowned." Barbara can still hear Charlotte's fluctuating voice but her thoughts continue back in time. "Another time Dad and Mom took us fishing down at the Saint Mary's River. The car was parked right on the edge of the riverbank when it started to rain. Mom and Dad continued fishing while all of us children waited in the car. Finally Dad decided we had better leave but because of the muddy ground, the car became bogged down and we couldn't move. It started to lean toward the water and we children became frightened. Charlotte, in her childlike wisdom, shouted 'Good God Almighty! Let's get out of here!' Dad eventually called Granddaddy Kurts who came with his truck, put us in the back, and took us to his house for the night."

Barbara still smiles at the incident while watching Charlotte's animated hand movements. "Charlotte always had unusually large eyes. As children we used to make fun of her and call her Bug-eyes. Actually, Charlotte has the prettiest eyes of all us sisters. Her best features are her eyes and thin lips. She is also a very loving person and has a wonderful gift of helping others; she always goes the extra mile. There seems to be a reversal of roles between us; she is more like my big sister rather than me being the eldest. She is always worrying about me as I drive to and from Indianapolis, checking on me to see if I made it okay. That's my sis, Charlotte." Barbara's reminiscing makes her feel like dozing. "Maybe I'll try to sleep some more. It makes a trip seem to go faster."

Marcia, always known as Marsha Wetter, feels somewhat removed from the chatter and laughter at the front of the van. Seated in the very rear diagonally from Barbara, she looks up from her crossword puzzle book. Her gaze lingers on Barbara as she notices that everyone else seems involved in something except for Barbara who is snoozing comfortably. "As far back as I can remember," Marcia reflects, "Barbara was always our second mother. When Mama would leave to go someplace she left Barb in charge. If we had to know something, we would ask her. She would tell us what she thought was best at that time and when Mom came home she would just ask if it was the right answer or if she did the right thing. To me, she was always closest to Mom. I tried to keep up with Barbara and do the things she did. She was the only one of us who accomplished playing a musical instrument, the clarinet, in public. I tried playing the xylophone, as it was called back then, but couldn't stick with it. Daddy always taught us to do the best we could do and that's the best we could do. I know Barb tried a lot harder than me and I admire her for it.

"I can remember us walking all the way to Northside High School in the cold of winter for the basketball games when Barbara played in the band. I was so proud of her and really wanted to see her more than the game. Mom always turned to the Lord for all of her answers and now that she's not here Barbara has stepped easily into her shoes. I used to think her standards were too high and I couldn't follow them. That's probably why I hung out with Charlotte more often. Barb was never an outgoing or demanding person. She only tried to mother us in Mom's absence. I remember a time when Mom was gone and a big storm came up. Barb had us all go into the basement and sit on the steps. Wow! After the storm was over, we came up to find that a large tree had fallen through our front window." With a sigh, Marcia returns her attention to her puzzle.

Those Holland Kids

In the front of the van the conversation comes to a lull. Charlotte turns to check out the activity in the rear. Directly behind her in the far right corner Marcia seems contentedly engrossed in something. Charlotte smiles to herself. "Why can't I be that way? Marcia can get comfortable like no one else I know. She hasn't made a peep in quite a while. Marcia, my darling sis, never seems to age even though she is the second eldest in the family." Charlotte remembers Marcia as a young girl. "She was always quiet, most of the time only talking when someone spoke first to her. She never seemed to think much about her position of being next to the eldest by lording over the younger siblings with demands and reprimands. She was very fond of her sisters and brothers and could be found often carting them around on her hip, especially Linda, the baby twin. Marcia has always gone about life in her own quiet way. But she is definitely not a pushover; quite the contrary. I remember a time when some of the neighborhood boys were picking on Jenny as we were heading home from a day of picking at the crabapple trees around our neighborhood, apron-like skirts loaded with the fruits of our labor. Marcia dropped her skirt and lit into those fellows sending them fleeing for their lives. There were also times when we all had to retreat to the sofa kicking up our heels to ward off Marcia's blows. We understood early on that it didn't pay to make her angry.

"In high school, Marcia was named 'Miss Sharp Dresser.' One of her favorite duos was a straight black pencil skirt with a powder blue sweater. She had the figure to wear it, too. She had a natural talent inherited from Mom of sewing. Today she is very talented at putting things together. She left the nest early compared to the rest of us girls when she married Wilma. She has raised seven children and has a host of grandchildren. But even with all those kids around, she is still 'quiet Marcia'.

"As I remember Jessie, known as Twerp, she was a quiet child as well, never loud spoken. I remember her being very sickly. Mom and Dad didn't know what her problem was. There was a doctor who lived across the street named Dr. Borders. He was so light-complexioned and white haired I remember being puzzled as to whether he was black or Caucasian. Anyway, Mom and Dad called him to come over and see about Jessie. After that she seemed to get better. The only thing was she never gained any weight. She stayed so thin Daddy nicknamed her Skinny Bones. I always felt like I was a second mother to her and Ken.

"Donna, who we named Lucy Locket, was another of my siblings I helped to raise. While Mom and Dad worked I had to make baby formula and take care of them. When Mom and Dad took time out to go somewhere in the evenings, I had to babysit. Well, anyway, Donna was a very pretty baby. She had those big slanted eyes that were dark like a little Jewish baby; she was so pretty. I would dress her up and sit her in the window as if she were a doll so people would see her as they passed by the house. I can't remember anything about her weaknesses except that when she grew older she would talk so much she sounded like a magpie. Those dark eyes would really flash. Daddy evidently saw something unusually promising in her. Maybe it was because she was the seventh child. He was right. She was, and still is, so knowledgeable in business. She is a real go-getter."

Settling into the placidity of the moment, Charlotte is enjoying her mental travels back in time. "Oh, how I wish Ken would join us for this great reunion. Kenny, the first male child in the Holland clan, was that long-awaited boy of Daddy's. He came along sixth in line after five girls. He started off in life loving to eat and falling down a lot, hurting himself and earning the nickname Butchie from his scars and Bread Snapper from being hungry all the time. He would get out of bed early in the morning when most of us children were still asleep, sit by the air vent to the downstairs, and whine to Mama and Daddy, 'Can I have a piece of bread?'

"When Butchie was a teenager, he was known to all the girls as 'the handsome dude.' His tall, slim frame, keen features, and golden complexion made him the 'spittin' image' of Daddy. And just like Kenneth Sr., he was very agile and up on all the latest dance steps. He was one of the popular dancers on the local TV version of American Bandstand. After graduating from high school, Kenny joined the U.S. Air Force and made it a career. He did maintenance on aircraft, a very important and responsible job. Like his dad, Kenneth Sr., he is a multi-talented person; he can do just about anything. He can fix things and build things, a jack-of-all-trades in every sense of the word. Kenny is retired now and continues a semi-quiet life in Arizona, singing karaoke from time to time at various restaurants and functions. I can hear his mellow Johnny Mathis-type voice, still in good tune after all these years."

Jessie's reading is making her feel somewhat drowsy. Looking up from the

Those Holland Kids

account of Jeremiah in the Bible on her lap, her thoughts drift as she settles back to relax in the very left rear of the van directly across from Marcia. "How perfect it would be if both Leonard and Linda could be with us this week. My dear baby twin brother and sister: even though they're nearing forty-one years old, they are still Baby Bro and Baby Sis to me.

"I remember so clearly when they were really young. They were, and still are, complete opposites in character. Leonard was always tinkering with mechanical things. He literally made a telephone out of a broken radio and hooked it up to the telephone line. It really worked! The phone company came out and disconnected it. My little brother was awesome. He could usually be found by himself creating something so not one of us was ever very close to him. It certainly makes sense to me that he later worked in the aerodynamics Industry. Yep, Baby Bro is still distant and mysterious.

"I helped Linda a lot with her homework. Marcia favored Linda and took a lot of time with her as well. Even though she really struggled in school, Linda has a lot of abilities that I never thought she'd possess such as her writing. She, too, tends to keep to herself and usually doesn't accompany us in our travels.

"As for me, Twerp, I always felt loved at home. My childhood was truly 'The Wonder Years.' Later I was told that the devil tried to 'take me out' when I was growing up. I was dropped on my head when I was only a baby. I was very ill at a young age with what might have been scarlet fever. Doctor Borders came to the house and was very concerned about me. I'm not sure if even he knew the seriousness of the case at that time. But years later, as an adult when I moved to Indianapolis, a doctor listened to my heart and asked me if I had ever had scarlet fever. I told him no.

"Anyway, I was very shy from my early youth even into young adulthood. I was always so skinny I got called Bones, Skinny Legs, and all that. Even though I was not ugly and had long pretty hair, it made me withdraw and feel very insecure. In high school, Mom always dressed us nice. My name was often in the school paper as one of those who wore sharp clothes. But I still felt shy.

"My nature, being a Melancholy and a striving perfectionist, caused me to be self-conscious. I felt I had to think everything out before I said anything to make sure I would say everything right. About time I got through thinking and pondering, the conversation would have passed on to the next issue (smile).

"I'll never forget how I used to feel when we sisters would gather over at Mom's. We'd all be sitting around talking. When I would make a comment and eyes turned to me I would start to stutter and sweat. I kid you not. I was pitiful.

"I remained that way until the Lord jumped in and called me to head up the Youth Department at McKee. I literally told the Lord surely He had the wrong person. Finally I said yes and that was the beginning of my breakthrough. Then He had me directing the Youth Choir. I see now that He was setting me up for my next phase: marrying a minister. Oh, my!

"I'm still conservative today even as a pastor's wife. I don't like a lot of attention. But the Lord has given me boldness when I need it. Now I can go up to anyone and feel confident in speaking because I know it's Him and not me. I am also more outspoken about things I believe in. I'm learning to say no more often, especially to telemarketers, etc. I'm still very self-conscious about my thin legs but I no longer let it hold me back.

Jessie smiles as her thoughts continue. "Now Donna, precious Donna, I miss her so much. We should be nearing Atlanta. It'll be so nice to see her again. We used to call her Lucy Lockett because Lucy was her nickname and her favorite cut-out doll, which she carried around with her all the time, was named Lucy Lockett. As she grew out of her baby beauty, I used to think Donna was a strange-looking child. She had a light streak down her nose. It was a birthmark, but it resembled a mark on the nose of Silver, Gene Autry's horse. We used to tease her about it. She would cry and fly into us, her arms swinging. She was quite a little spitfire. When she got really angry the white streak really showed up. But she had a lovely wide smile whenever she wasn't angry.

"Daddy repeatedly told us Donna was going to grow up and be a beauty. We would all break out laughing and said, 'No way!' How right Daddy was. She began showing this beauty in her late teens. Donna also has many other attributes. She's talented, very determined, successful, elegant, and beautiful."

Startled, Jessie's mind returns to the present. Suddenly anxious for the long journey from Indianapolis to end, she asks, "How close are we now?"

Grateful for the stirring up of the atmosphere since everyone seems to have fallen into the quiet realm of either peaceful thought or light sleep, Cecelia says, "Almost to 285. Someone had better call Donna for directions."

Marcia, in the middle of a difficult cryptogram, listens to the conversation about directions and traffic conditions and decides to jump in. "It's going to be wonderful seeing Debra, my grandchildren, and my great grandchildren while I'm here," she says. "And it feels so good being away from my job."

Barbara is barely listening to the chatter, again engrossed in searching for her habitually disappearing glasses. "Thank God we're almost there," she thinks. "I'm really ready for the bed. I wonder how George is going to deal with my absence for a whole week, cooking his own meals and having no one to pester" (chuckle, chuckle). Being the eldest and most sober of all the sisters, Barbara would never speak such thoughts aloud but she savors her humor privately.

Wide awake and comfortably wearing her traffic engineer's hat, Charlotte does what comes naturally for her; being Cecelia's eyes, ears, and roadmap as the Mercury van slows and becomes one with the Marietta southbound rush-hour traffic.

In Atlanta, Donna hangs up the phone feeling a mixture of excitement and anxiety. "Yippie! They're coming to Atlanta, all my dear sisters. How I look forward to this special time of doing nothing except sitting around and chitchatting about the past, the Word of God, and Biblical Prophecy, simply having fun, fun, fun. I miss them so very much. I'll never get the rest of this stuff finished before they get here, there are so many loose ends still hanging. They'll be hungry so there's homemade soup on the stove, a special gourmet pasta dish prepared, and of course, sweet potato pies baking in the oven. There's no time now to worry about anything except getting myself dressed.

"Our very first sister-reunion! I can just imagine Jessie will be first out of the van and up the walkway. How close we used to be when we were growing up! Even though we were total opposites in personality we were always like two peas in a pod; hugged up together whenever we went roller-skating or to church. Jessie was very shy. I think it was because she felt she was too skinny so she withdrew for reasons of insecurity. I, too, was very skinny and self-conscious, but I think my attitude was more in the realm of 'I'll do all I can to hide my skinny legs with longer skirts, etc'.

"Jessie was very pretty with sparkling eyes and got all the attention from the boys. She had a cute shape and a nice little butt. I, on the other hand, had nothing to look at in that capacity. Jessie was very conservative in her dress and didn't like a lot of attention. Me, I craved attention so I dressed a little livelier and talked a little louder. I think it was because I never felt really loved as a child. Yes, we went everywhere together and even though we grew up in church and Sunday school, we also tried being a little adventurous.

"I remember one night when we were young adults we made the drastic decision to 'go out,' as we called it. We headed to a local bar to have fun. We were all dressed up to kill (we thought). It was raining cats-n-dogs out. In the car we were laughing and talking. Jessie was paying too little attention to her driving and went right through a red traffic light. We both saw the police car some distance behind us at the same time. We quickly put our youthful minds together and made the decision to turn down some alleyways and short streets before the patrol car could get turned around. Since it was nighttime it would be easy enough to ditch him. Pulling into our destination we were laughing victoriously only to find in the rearview mirror that we had company. The shiny blue patrol car pulled up right behind us. We rolled down our windows. The smiling officer asked us what we were trying to do and told us he simply followed our tire tracks on the wet pavement. We were too stunned by our ignorance. The officer turned out to be someone who knew our entire Holland family. He warned us that he would report our little shenanigan to Mother if we ever tried that stunt again.

Those Holland Kids

"Well, that was then. Today Jessie and I are two women who love the Lord with heart and soul. Jessie has a wonderful gift of being able to exhibit that love to everyone she knows and meets. She also has a gift for appreciating music and art. She enjoys the beauty of nature, reading, sketching, painting, and studying. We are both melancholy personalities so we strive for perfectionism and—

"Oh, my! They're here and I'm not even finished dressing."

With a loud sigh of triumph, Cecelia turns into the driveway of the three-story wood-frame house on Ridgedale Way. Situated at the main entrance corner of the subdivision, the pale blue-gray structure surrounded by azaleas in full bloom and dogwood trees are a welcome sight. A stately row of red tipped shrubbery offers just enough shade for Cecelia's van. As usual, everyone is talking at the same time as they search for personal belongings. Charlotte can't seem to find her purse and Barbara is still missing her glasses. Jessie leads the pack as the first to reach the door. Her "Hellooooo, Sis, how are you?" is met with a big bear hug. As usual, Cecelia livens the grand entrance with her unique way of saying hello: "Child, what's wrong with your head? You look like Aunt Ja'noonie (Cecelia's own imaginary creation of Aunt Jemima's sister).

Cecelia has gained too many extra pounds over the years, but that has never slowed her down very much. It certainly has not detracted from her beauty. Her thick, long, black, curly hair is tied back and swirled perfectly into a large knot, complimenting her oval face. She's not smiling as she speaks her usual light-hearted insults, but somehow her sisters know it's all in fun and are openly humored by it. The grand welcome, many hugs, and much food bring the day to a peaceful but exhausting close. The seventy-five-degree Georgia sun begins its descent behind the horizon with varying hues of orange, red, and brown.

The next morning Jessie lies in bed as the sun's rays work their way around the corners of the drawn shades and pale yellow chemise curtains. "What a wonderful evening we had. The food was superb and we had a glorious time reminiscing about old times on Brackenridge Street where we grew up. I know I should get up and join the bunch in the kitchen but I'm gonna treat myself to the few extra winks I greatly deserve. My jobs as pastor's wife, grandma of twelve, secretary for the church, and business manager for Tom's auto repair shop are sometimes more than I can handle. But it's also becoming a real test to lay here with all of the good-smelling aromas coming up from the kitchen."

Drifting somewhere between a light slumber and a well-deserved relaxed state, Jessie begins remembering the testimony she shared with the family about "how great is our God." She had written a letter and sent it to each of her sisters.

"Hello everyone,

As some of you already know, I was under a severe attack over the last month. My obligations and schedules had gotten completely out of hand. My calendar was so full that it looked more like graffiti than a calendar. Seriously! I didn't want to even THINK about another date obligation.

"There were a lot of other things going on, as well and I was almost at my wit's end. I was contemplating packing my bags and running off. But my Father in heaven saw this pitiful creature and had compassion on her.

"September first, which was Labor Day, I had a dream. I was walking down Brackenridge Street, toward Mom's house. There were many people around the neighborhood and things were in chaos. It seemed there had been a tornado or something and people were praying. I began searching for Mom and finally spotted her on the side of the house. She was stooped over, picking up paper from the lawn. She had on a white dress with pale blue flowers around the bodice and along the pockets of the skirt. She looked like an angel; when I saw her, I thought, 'That's just like my Mom, always doing something nice, even in the midst of turmoil and trouble.' When she stood up, she saw me and gave me a big smile. I raced up to her, threw my arms around her and hugged her tight. My heart was overflowing with love for her. "Oh Mom", I said. "I love you so much!" *Then I began to weep. I couldn't hold back the tears, they just flowed. She never said a word, only just embraced me tenderly. I laid my head on her shoulder and I wanted to pour out all my frustrations that were bottled up inside of me.*

"I woke up and was still weeping. I continued to feel the warmth of her arms around me. I wanted to wake up Tom and ask him to just hold me. Instead, I got up

wondering who I would call. Since it was so early, Barbara came to my mind. I knew she'd be bright and chipper (smile). I called her and poured out my heart to her. She listened intently, much like Mom. She gave me some wise counsel and then prayed for me. Oh my! Mom's mantle has truly fallen on Barb, and she has no idea because of her humble spirit.

"I know you all remember what a prayer warrior Mom was. Whenever I went to her with my problems, she would just listen and every now and then give her soft expressions of 'Oh my,' or 'That's too bad,' or something of that nature. She would then pray for me. There was one thing I was very confident about. When she began her prayer with 'Oh Lord,' I knew she had his full attention. Mom's prayers were always so very genuine. She took her time and talked to Him the same way she talked to us. When she finished praying I knew everything was going to be alright.

"I thank God for my breakthrough that Monday morning. I am also thankful to Him for that sweet and beautiful dream of Mom that stayed with me for several days. I also thank him for you, my family. I love you all.

"I can say, without reservations, that I am a blessed woman to have been born into this wonderful family. And I want to thank you all for the love you have shown me throughout my life. Mom would be so proud to see what all of her prayers and tears, I'm certain, have accomplished in her children.

"I pray that this has blessed you as it has blessed me. I can hardly wait until the day we have that Grand Reunion in heaven. God bless you all! I love you all so very, very much!

> As Always, Your Sis,
> Jess (Twerp)"

"I know I should get up and join the breakfast bunch, but for some reason, I can't stop my thoughts about Mom. I can see her face so clearly. I always thought Mom's features resembled an Indian, especially her nose. She was very pretty and most of the time she had a smile on her face. She was a tall, large-boned, brown-skinned woman.

"Mom was quiet-spirited and very soft-spoken. When she was led to talk she was full of Godly Wisdom. Whenever she was worried or deep in thought you could see the soft lines in her forehead more clearly (which we were often responsible for). Though we were very poor, Mom never complained. She was reserved, private, and had very few close friends even though she was loved and popular with neighbors and church members. Being a preacher's daughter, she made sure we went to church every Sunday.

"I remember Mom spending a lot of time in the kitchen. She had a habit of doing her cooking while wearing only an under-slip top and skirt. We used to sing with her while we all did the chores. She had a beautiful alto voice. When we sang the song, If You Only Knew, Mom sang alto, I sang tenor, and Cecelia sang soprano. The harmony was awesome. 'If you only knew... the depth of God's love... If you only knew... Christ came from above... He came to save sinners... condemned by the fall... each lost son of Abraham... who'll answer His call... If you only knew... If you only knew....'

"Many days when we came home from school the evidence of Mom being in the kitchen met us as we approached the house. There were the familiar aromas of muffin bread, steamed rutabagas, and oxtail stew. Other days we would be disappointed when we ran into the house only to take in the smell of dirty clothes being washed in the old wringer washer in the kitchen.

"After Daddy died, the obligations of taking care of the house and providing for nine children became overwhelming for her. During those days, I am ashamed to say, I did not think much about what she was going through or how difficult it had to be for her. Mom was a woman of limited education, but was a very hard worker. She was always busy doing something. I can't ever remember coming home from school to find her lying around sleeping or reading. She would, however, have the radio tuned to her favorite soaps, Stella Dallas or The Edge of Night.

"Oh, my!" Jessie says, finally overcome by the mixture of pleasant odors from downstairs. "I had best get up."

In the kitchen, Barbara pours her second cup of coffee while Charlotte spreads butter on her blueberry bran muffin. Cecelia passes around the redskin hash brown potatoes and Marcia enjoys her perfectly-browned Bob Evans sausage links. Jessie enters the kitchen and heads directly toward the hot water and tea. Taking a minute to relax, Donna sits next to Cecelia. "Let's talk about where we're going tonight," she says excitedly.

Later, savoring the aftereffects of the typical grand breakfast served whenever anyone came to Donna's house, each person settles into her chosen spot for quiet time. Marcia chooses an isolated seat out on the deck near the birdbath and water fountain, her crossword puzzle book in hand. Barbara relaxes on the den sofa with her Bible study materials. Cecelia retreats to the bedroom to make her traditional rounds of telephone calls to each of her children back home in Indiana. Jessie, like Marcia, takes advantage of the pleasant, not-too-hot sunshine and settles for the front porch to take in the neighbor's art of floral planting and landscaping. Donna hasn't wound down yet and takes the time to get the last of the laundry folded and put away.

Charlotte finds a quiet place on the plush, muted berry-colored lounger off of the living area giving her a clear view of the rear landscape through the dining room picture window. As she reaches for her carry-all bag on the floor next to her feet for something to read, the beauty of Georgia catches her eye causing her to pause to appreciate the extravaganza of colors. Pink and purple dogwood blossoms with their dark red stems make a vivid demonstration of contrast against the yellow, gold, and orange hues of the oak leaves. The captivating red and salmon-colored azalea blossoms make a striking statement alongside the thick, glossy, red foliage.

The serene splendor and tranquility of the late-morning sun quickly changes Charlotte's mood to one of complete relaxation. The events of the day, the long drive in the van with her sisters, and this first reunion have begun to stir memories of the past; childhood memories, some good and some not so good. Charlotte muses, "As I consider all our family has endured it makes me realize we are a family of survivors because Mom was a survivor. And in a world where close-knit families are just not popular anymore, being here with most of my sisters really warms my heart.

"I can't help remembering when we were children at our little house and home on Brackenridge Street. We kids and Daddy would sit on the front steps at night. The smaller ones would stretch out on their backs looking up at the stars. Daddy would explain to us how these days were the best of our lives and we should savor and enjoy them to the fullest. I remember thinking, 'What is he talking about? All I want to do is grow up and move on.' Oh, Daddy, how right you were!

"I can see him almost as clearly as I saw him nearly fifty years ago. Daddy was a very handsome man with keen features. He was fair-skinned, tall and slender, with close-cut wavy hair. The thin mustache he wore added to his charming looks, which he was very particular about. He would spend extra time at the mirror making certain every hair was in its proper place.

"Daddy's strongest character trait was that he was very proper and mannerly in his speech. He was intelligent and quite knowledgeable about world affairs. He spoke of things that would take place or come to pass in the future, things our little minds found hard to believe or imagine. He could do seemingly anything. He was also a jack-of-all-trades, and to us, master of them all.

"He dearly loved music and passed that love on to us children. He made piano lessons available to each one of us as soon as we were able to read. We all loved it. We would be fascinated and excited as we watched him play the xylophone for us. He was extremely talented and would thrill us by using two or three mallets in each hand. I loved music from day one and remember Daddy lifting each one of us up onto a chair while teaching us to play that monstrous instrument. When we were older, we had to disassemble and reassemble the xylophone many times and carry it around for him to different musical events. Good thing Daddy had us kids to help him since we didn't have an automobile at that time (smile). I bet we looked a sight walking down the streets (in a line, no doubt) carrying parts of that xylophone (ha ha!). Yes, those were the days!

"There were also special times when he would play records on the phonograph. He, Mom, and we older girls would sit for hours listening to Chet Baker, Sarah Vaughan, and other jazz artists. The little ones would be there, too, not understanding who those jazz icons were, but absorbing and enjoying the arts. It's no small wonder we all continue to love music in one aspect or another. Some of us love to sing or dance; some of us still play the piano. We all have an ear for music and just simply enjoy listening to smooth jazz artists. Yes, those were the days, those early days when music filled our home at

Those Holland Kids

526 E. Brackenridge Street. They were the happiest times for us from the days when Daddy and Mom sat and judged our many talent shows to the day he brought home the first record player to the times when piano, xylophone, clarinet, and other music radiated from that little house."

Donna makes her way through the upstairs hallway into her bedroom. She finally slows down enough to admit to herself aloud, "I am totally exhausted. Why, oh, why is it that I always do this to myself? Whenever anyone tells me they are coming I begin my crazy mission of non-stop preparations. Everything has to be perfect: the house, the food, the entertainment, and the sightseeing." She falls backward onto the bed muttering to herself. "I'll just lay here for a few minutes while I decide what time we need to get started for our evening of fun.

"This will be a great preview of a wonderful fun-filled week. I have to remind myself often, though, not to talk too much or crack too many jokes. I tend to take over conversations and give my opinions on every subject. When our time together has ended and everyone is gone I don't want to spend the next few weeks wallowing in regret. No, no! I won't go there this time.

"Cecelia, on the other hand, won't be restrained. She'll keep us all rolling in laughter. Since I am one of the youngest of the family, I remember Cecelia's younger years only from often-told stories. Cecelia—I have always called her Jenny—was the fourth and the most vibrant of the lot. She was somewhat big for her age, but not overweight, just large-boned. She stood out in so many ways; she was the only one of us with skin the color of a Caucasian and with completely black naturally curly hair. They say she had a 'tiger in the tank,' constantly in trouble for one thing or another. She didn't care how she looked so her hair was always all over her head, flying in the wind. She preferred running barefoot. Whenever her wild misbehavior resulted in Daddy getting involved he had to deal out her retributions in the 'big closet' to muffle her screams. It wasn't that Daddy was overly abusive, but Jenny's yelling was much louder than the rest. That was apparently how she liked to react; it seemed to fit her personality.

"During my teen years I became closer to Cecelia than to my other sisters. Jessie, my spiritual twin and buddy, was already married. Barbara, Charlotte, and Marcia were either out on their own or married. Linda and

Leonard were too young and Kenny had gone off to the Air Force. So it was just me, Cecelia, and Mom. During that time Mom wasn't herself emotionally so Cecelia watched over me. I like to think back on the time when she bought me a small wardrobe of clothes. I was so excited! There were pretty skirts, blouses, a sweater, and some shoes. To me, that was a wardrobe. I remember thinking I was the cutest girl in school. Then Cecelia took me to the Links Skating Rink. I wore my pink floral skirt and solid pink blouse. I danced around like a little madwoman right in front of my enemies, the girls who hated me. They just sat and glared at me while I pranced all around them. They dared not touch me because Jenny was never too far away. She was big, tall, and strong.

"Jenny has such a giving heart and I know she loved me, her little sis. Years later when Cecelia was dating Poogie, her third husband, I was married with children. Cecelia and Poogie would meet and hang out at the VFW Lodge around the corner from where I lived. Our relationship took a drastic turn. She and Poogie argued a lot and I was afraid they would come to blows and Jenny would get hurt so I became her guardian angel. I found myself following her around thinking I could somehow protect her. I was even having a hard time sleeping at night. As I think back, and picture the scenario, Poogie was a stocky 5' 5" tall. Cecelia was a strong and solid 5' 10" and I was a scrawny 5' 6". I don't think I weighed more than 90 pounds. But amazingly, they never came to blows and my deepest fears were unfounded. Thank you, Lord!

"As time went by, several major events took place in Cecelia's life and in mine. Our differences became magnified. We found ourselves constantly at great odds with each other. There were things that were her fault, and there were definitely things that were my fault. Nevertheless, our relationship suffered and only became worse whenever we were in each others' presence. I really believe, looking back, that because we were so different in lifestyle, we didn't click. But because we were so much alike in personality, we clashed. I still walk on eggshells whenever we're around each other. Lord, help me to mind my big mouth so as not to cause friction between us. Taking my request a step further, if there are any issues this week please don't let me be the villain!"

chapter

2

(three days later)
Distressing realities
of the past

The shiny new van with Cecelia at the wheel moves at a steady pace northbound on Interstate 75 towards Chattanooga. Seated in her same place at the far right rear of the van behind Charlotte, Marcia's mind is a rollercoaster of thoughts from exuberance days earlier to the surprise and disappointment that followed.

"The tension in the quietness of this vehicle is so thick if I had a knife I could probably cut it into slices," Marcia mutters under her breath. "This is terrible! Our very first sister-reunion; what a disaster!" She revisits how she felt en route to Atlanta. "I was so excited looking forward to being with my sisters, so happy I felt on the verge of being ecstatic. Since I was the first to get married I hadn't been able to spend quality time with any one of them in years. After being separated from them by my family priorities at a very young age this reunion time was just what I needed.

"I took snapshots of us in front of Donna's house with plans of framing them. I appreciate how Donna opened up her beautiful home to us and made us all so comfortable. We sat around talking, eating, and viewing old photos of when we were kids; it was awesome. Also, it was the first time I had ever been to Atlanta so I thoroughly enjoyed the tour of the city. Donna took us to a health food store and I bought herbal teas I didn't even know existed. We dined at vegetarian restaurants where the food was absolutely delicious; we were having a grand time together. Everything was going wonderfully until we went to Underground Atlanta.

"All the nicer eating establishments were filled except for one called Mick's. It was very popular and we were looking forward to sampling the unique menu of specialty foods, everyone except Jenny. She was adamant about not going in there because they served alcohol. No amount of reasoning with her changed her mind. We explained that we would not be drinking, that the bar was far removed from where we would be seated, and that most of the nicer restaurants served alcohol. Nothing budged Jenny in the least. In fact, the more we tried convincing her, the more firmly she planted her feet and dug in her heels.

"Charlotte became very upset. And she didn't bite her tongue in expressing what she felt about Jenny's phobia. She pointed out that Jenny was overreacting. The dramatic situation finally ended with Jenny leaving the restaurant. Jessie went with her and they ate somewhere else. The silent war was on: Charlotte and Jenny (Cecelia) were highly upset with each other."

Marcia's thoughts continued. "Back at Donna's house, Jenny began preaching to us all as we sat around the kitchen table. Just when we thought or hoped she would calm down she announced that she was going home. She gathered her belongings and informed us, 'Ladies, whoever is going with me had better get your bags in the van or you will be walking back to Indiana.'

All of our eyes popped open wide. 'What?' Charlotte spoke up. 'You can't mean that! We're not leaving tonight, surely.' 'Oh, yes we are,' Cecelia flung back.

"Yes, our first sister reunion started out like a sleeping lamb, but it ended like a roaring lion. Little Jenny, Captain Wild Woman as we called her in our childhood days, showed up again. It was as though we were kids once more and Jenny owned the ball we were playing with. Jenny got mad at us so she took the ball and went home. She would just leave us all in the lurch if need be since we were traveling in her van. Even though we have always loved one another as siblings we haven't always been able as adults to relate to one another's personality traits."

The sudden blare of the tape player jolted Marcia out of her melancholy thoughts. Two seats ahead of her in the front passenger seat Charlotte laid down her book and glared at Cecelia out of the corner of her eye without turning her head. "Oh, Lord!" Charlotte mutters to herself. "I hope this crazy wild child doesn't repeat what she did when we left home coming to Atlanta. We were having such fun in her shiny new well-equipped van, watching television, listening to truckers on the CB radio, and laughing at her jokes. Then all of a sudden, Jenny began raving about her pastor. She said he had some Biblical insights she wanted to share with us so she put in a tape and turned the volume up. To me, the preaching was very boring and his message was way out in left field. It went on and on until some of us just ignored it and began conversing among ourselves. It became obvious this upset Cecelia but she eventually turned it off and the rest of the trip went smoothly.

"Now here she goes again, the same tape, the same message, and the same pastor. The only difference is the volume; she has it blasting. I guess she's making sure we hear every word this time. It sounds like the message is aimed at us misguided believers to make us see the light of the truth." Charlotte chuckles at her private joke. "We all attend churches of different denominations but that has never posed a problem for any of us except for Cecelia. She has always believed her faith is the only truth."

Charlotte glances over at Barbara sitting directly behind the driver's seat. Barbara looks up from the open Bible on her lap just in time to catch Charlotte's eye. Being the eldest, the most sober, and the most tolerant of the sisters, Barbara tries not to allow the turbulence in the air to change her mood. It does, however, stir up thoughts about the past in light of what just happened at Donna's and at Underground Atlanta. "Amazing," Barbara muses. "If I were a betting woman my money would have been on Jenny and Donna to be at each others' throats. What a switch-a-roo!

"Jenny's reaction to eating at the pub-style restaurant reminds me of her old lifestyle before she got saved. She used to hang out in liquor joints. She drank much too much and chain-smoked cigarettes for many years. It's very possible she thought she couldn't handle being reminded of her past by such a close encounter with the enemy.

"My prayer tonight, Lord, is that you somehow bring peace to this situation and calm all hearts from any bitterness or confusion." Barbara spoke more prayers to her Lord under her breath as she settled once again into her reading.

Four Days Later

Wednesday morning in Indianapolis brings a cool steady down-pouring of rain, a perfect day to spend indoors. Jessie pulls the soft fleece bed jacket up around her shoulders as she wiggles her way to a sitting position. "Why bother to get out of bed at all today?" Jessie mutters. The passing thought quickly turns into a brilliant idea. "Thomas is spending the day over at the church and I have the house all to myself. Why not?"

Jessie watches the wind in the trees outside her window and listens to the rain's patter against the pane. The heavy downpour subsides. She mulls over her experience in the middle of the night. She had not slept well. The trip home from Atlanta had seemed to take forever. She had tossed and turned trying to resist the urge to get up and pray. As usual, she finally gave in and followed her heart. After praying for some time she crawled back into her bed yet she still felt unable to sleep. She knew the Lord had endowed her with the gift of Peacemaking. She never could put up with violence or confusion. So she reached for the legal pad on the night table. Her mind still burdened with the way things took a wrong turn at their sister-reunion, Jessie picked up a pen and began pouring out her heart.

Oct. 12, 1995

To My Sisters,

It is now 4 a.m. and the Lord has laid on my heart to write this letter of encouragement. Tues. night the Lord gave me some things to share with you all. He knows I am a procrastinator by nature so He said this morning, "Get up now and do it!"

We all know that we are living in the "last days." Jesus is on His way back. Satan knows his days are numbered and that is why he and all his demons are working furiously to torment and destroy God's people.

Ephesians 5:11-17 warns us to put on the whole armor of God and resist the devil's strategies and stand our ground in the evil day. We are in the evil days.

II Corinthians 2:11 says, "...We are not ignorant of Satan's devices." Therefore, let's look at the "whole scenario" with our spiritual eyes. The only way we are going to make it through these terrible times, (and it's going to get worse) is by standing on, and doing, God's Word.

Eph. 6:11 in the Amplified Bible says, "(You) Put on God's whole armor, so that you may be able to stand up against (all) the strategies and the deceits of the devil." Vs. 12, "For we are not wrestling with flesh and blood but against powers, the rulers of the darkness of this present world, against spiritual wickedness in high places."

Sisters, we all acknowledged that our family is blessed. God's Mighty Hand has covered us through the years to this present time for some reason. It surely was not because of our goodness. The thought came in my heart that Mom might have made some type of covenant (agreement) with the Lord on our behalf.

We all know that Mom was a godly, praying woman. We also know that Mom loved us all sacrificially. (Barbara can confirm this.) We will never know this side of heaven what Mom prayed, after Daddy died, leaving her with nine children. We do know that part of her vow was to never allow us, her children, to be subjected to any kind of cruelty. That is why she never remarried.

Satan knows God has a plan for us and he's determined to thwart that plan. How? "United we stand, divided we fall."

We planned to have a family gathering every year this time. We were looking at meeting out West with our brothers next year. That was God's plan. But Satan said, "Oh yeah? I'll fix that!" Satan hates love, unity, peace, and the family structure. Need I say more?

To combat all our negative thoughts right now, we first of all need to pray for one another. Eph. 6:18 let's us know we have to intercede for one another because Satan is raging. He's mad and is out to destroy us all. Let's resist him.

The Lord reminded me that we had talked at one time about getting a Family Newsletter circulated amongst the family. This will help us to be brought up to date on what is happening in each family, plus help us to know and understand one another. Although we are family, we really do not "Know" one another because of distance, personal schedules, etc.

The newsletter will consist of articles, pictures, our beliefs our likes and dislikes, our quirks, mannerisms, phobias, and temperaments. Do you understand what I am saying?

When we were children, we were around each other day and night. We knew each other. But because we didn't know Jesus we fought like cats and dogs. (smile) Not all the time, because underneath it all, there was love.

All nine of Mom's children are different because God made us that way. We all have strengths and weaknesses. We are all important and fit in God's Plan. To get to know each other better, in this coming year, let's determine (with God's help) to call, write, visit one another. Let's find out what God has for us. It must be good or Satan would not be fighting so hard.

Also, the Lord let me know that a book is going to be written concerning our family. This will be a witness to the world of God's Almighty power and faithfulness.

So sisters, I close with this. Let's each examine our own heart and let the Holy Spirit do spiritual surgery where needed. James 3:13-18 says, "Who is a wise man and endued with knowledge among you? Let him show out of a good conversation (the way he lives) his works with meekness of wisdom.

"But if you have bitter envying and strife in your heart, glory not, and lie not against the truth."(Don't deceive yourself.) This wisdom comes not from above (from God) but is earthly, sensual, devilish, (from Satan).

"For where envying and strife is, there is confusion and every evil work. But the wisdom that is from above is first pure, then peaceable, gentle, and easy to be entreated, (yield to reason) full of mercy and good fruits, without partiality, and without hypocrisy.

"And the fruit of righteousness is sown in peace of them that make peace."

> Your Sis,
> Jessie Mae
> (Twet Twot Twerp)
> as Daddy used to call me
> (smile)

P.S.
I love you all very much.

P.P.S.
Would everyone try to get hold of the book, "Your Temperament: Discover Its Potential" by Tim LaHaye? It will help us all.

Monday Afternoon, October 21, 1995

Cecelia sits quietly with the pages of Jessie's letter that arrived in today's mail lying loose on her lap. She is a little surprised at how peaceful she feels after reading it despite the last several days of frustration. A smile begins forming on her lips. "Well, I guess I do owe everyone an apology. And isn't this just like Jessie? She never rests until we're all thoroughly convicted of our misdeeds." Her smile widens.

In the midst of her solitude, Cecelia feels a tear rolling down her cheek. "Why couldn't my childhood have been different? Why, oh, why did I cause Mom and Daddy so much trouble?" Almost as quickly as she sinks into remorse she remembers how gracious and merciful is the Lord Jesus Christ, her Savior. "He, after all, is in control and always has been.

"Don't really have an excuse for how I reacted to going into that restaurant. I guess it was just the thought of sitting in the middle of cigarette smoke and alcohol that made me kind of crazy. I dearly love all my sisters, and I especially have never liked to see my dear sis Bibba sad or frustrated. When we were all very young at home with Mom all Barb had to do was to look at us sternly. We got the message and straightened up.

"Oh, how I remember our little house and home on Brackenridge Street. I have always loved our address; 526 had a special ring about it. In a way, I was proud to give it out to people. It sounded sort of ritzy. By no means was our house any ways near being ritzy or classy or even beautiful. The brick streets were uneven in many places and the sidewalks were even bumpier. There were bricks missing with every step it seemed and dirt oozed out from in between covering the remaining bricks so they lost their original redness.

"The yard, likewise, was deprived of beautiful grass, beaten down by many little shoes and bare feet. Dirt was King of the Yards. Our back yard was especially horrible. But as children, we didn't consider it too bad. It was where we went after returning from the movies to act out what we had seen; Tarzan, Jane, or whatever. But as we grew so did the weeds. They were so thick and tall you could not find or see anything else. I, for the most part, was actually afraid to venture out in the back yard.

"The place that was our stage, so to speak, was the side porch. There were no banisters or posts, per se, just a concrete slab. It, too, was very unattractive, but we loved playing house on it. As we became older that side door became the main entrance in and out of the house. I hated that door because it never closed securely. And even more than the side door, I loathed our back door; it was in even worse shape. If anyone wanted to get in and do us harm they had an open invitation (in the natural realm, of course).

"Now, the inside of our house gave me some heart-warming pleasure. Even though it left a lot to be desired as well, my favorite place was the front room as we called it. It was the only part that was halfway decently furnished, the highlight being the piano and the xylophone. The middle room, what should have been the dining room, had a large pot-bellied coal-burning stove in it. The only other things in the middle room were Mom's sewing machine and some chairs. We all had to have a place to huddle on cold winter nights and it was around that ol' pot-bellied stove.

"The short hallway to the kitchen had a door that led to the basement. That definitely was a door I tried to ignore. I would only go down those steps when Mom ordered me and Charlotte to go down and get a bucket of coal. The front part had only one dim light. The floor was usually muddy from occasional flooding. Another room at the back had no door at all, only a big hole in the concrete wall. It was pitch black back there except during the daytime when light from outside filtered in around the coal chute.

"The only thing I liked about the kitchen was the good aromas that permeated the atmosphere when Mom was cooking. There were steps off the kitchen up to the two bedrooms. The front one was Mom and Daddy's and all of us kids slept in the back room two or three to a bed. We played musical beds most nights. The younger ones played there. When I got older, I loved to lie on the floor and daydream looking out the window that overlooked the porch side of the house.

"My goodness! I've drifted from Underground Atlanta to my childhood home and back. I'd better snap out of it and call everybody. I wonder if anyone else has read their letter."

At Barb's house, just around the corner from Cecelia's, she finishes reading Jessie's letter. "How timely," Barbara concludes. "We really need this spiritual boost. Like Jessie, I believe this is an opportune time to launch our family newsletter. Matter of fact, I'll arrange a conference call meeting so we can get it off the ground. Daddy would be so pleased if he were here. Even now, I believe he's smiling down upon us along with Mom."

The thought of Daddy causes Barbara's emotional high to begin its descent. She remembers when Daddy was hospitalized with what was later found to be meningitis. "Upon his initial release, medical doctors didn't know what caused his mental and physical downward spiral. He had become a different person altogether. Gone was the tall, handsome, intelligent Daddy we had always known and admired. He walked with a stoop. His face took on a wide-eyed, mentally retarded look. His previously meticulous and proper way of communicating gave way to stammering, repetitive foolishness. I was afraid to be around him and also, in my childish ignorance, ashamed of him.

"One time Daddy jumped on the recreation bus going out to the skating rink with me and my friends. When we got there, Daddy put on skates and proceeded to stumble around the rink, falling down numerous times giggling like a madman. I wanted to go through the floor.

"Shortly afterward, Mom had to have him committed to an insane asylum (as we called it back then) in Richmond. The travesty of the entire matter is that in those days medical doctors commonly mistook spinal meningitis for insanity. I remember how in my teens I felt I had to go see what I could do to get Daddy released. They did let me in to visit him, but that was all I could accomplish. We sat together in the dark, dismal visitors' area. Daddy made statements to me suggesting that the aides and caretakers were being abusive to him. They were also giving him electric shock treatments, the accepted procedure in those days for the mentally ill.

"Daddy kept asking me to do what I could to get him out of that place. He said if he didn't get out of there now, later it would only be because he was dead. I told him I would go to the office and talk to them. The head doctor told me because I was underage I wouldn't be able to sign him out. I left the office and walked out into the bright sunlight. As I passed by Daddy's building, en route to the bus line, I looked up to see him watching me from a small window that overlooked the long, winding walkway. I waved at him. I will never forget the pitiful look on his face. That picture haunted me for a long time. I even had dreams about it.

"It was in that asylum where Daddy died. His room had been on the second floor at the top of a horrible, dangerous-looking flight of wood and metal steps. They said he fell and broke his hip. It was believed one of the caretakers caused him to fall down those treacherous stairs.

"I don't remember ever having any conversation with Mom about Daddy's situation. She may have been afraid to get him out because of his mental condition, I really don't know. What I do know is that Daddy is in Glory now. When he was in another city before he was admitted to the facility in Richmond he wrote Mom a letter. Someone had witnessed to him and he received Jesus Christ as his personal Savior. He sounded very excited about it. Whatever issues Mom and Daddy ever had I know they were resolved because Mom always talked about going home to be with Jesus and Kenny. Mom always called Daddy, Kenny."

Regurgitating the entire episode of her father's slow decline to his last days on earth leaves Barbara feeling drained. Sighing, she concludes, "It always affects me like this." With an overwhelming anxiousness inside her to go ahead and get this family newsletter started, she picks up the phone to call Jessie.

chapter 3

May 31, 1996
A dream come true; the first family newsletter

With excitement and anticipation, Jessie pulls a large envelope from the mailbox. "Praise God," she says aloud. "Our very first family newsletter is in my hands. This is literally my dream and heart's desire come true. It means so much to me I can hardly wait to find a quiet place and time to sit and get into it."

After the dinner dishes are cleared and Tom has gone over to the church, Jessie sets the teapot on the stove. "I'll reread the letter from Charlotte that sparked the initial idea of a newsletter to keep in touch with each other," she says out loud. "Then I'll enjoy our first issue along with a cup of tea."

She settles on the deck outside the kitchen, opens the letter, and begins to read it once again.

February 26, 1996

Dear Sisters & Brothers:

Do you recognize this date, February 26? Yes, this is Mom's birth date. This was the one day of the year our family came together to celebrate. Those were wonderful times, weren't they? We would always put together some sort of entertainment for Mom. And she loved anything and everything we did for her. She would always giggle and keep saying things like, "Oh my goodness!" What a sweet, sweet mother we had!

The thought just popped into my mind, shortly after I woke up this morning, that we must do everything we can to keep The Holland Family together. Life is so busy, now, and I believe it is Satan's strategy to keep people (especially families) apart. But we will not let him succeed, as far as our family is concerned.

God gave me the idea, I'm sure, to have a monthly family newsletter. This will keep everyone abreast of how each of us is doing. We all have good intentions to call each other often, but we not only get busy and bogged down, it is also expensive.

Of course, I can't call everyone each month to gather your news for each issue. So, I will depend on each of you to send me your information, by the first week of the month. The newsletter will be mailed out to you on the 26th of the month.

Your information should consist of:

Those Holland Kids

- anything you want to share with the family
- what has taken place in your life
- what plans you have or what's coming up
- what your kids are doing
- etc., etc

Your info can be any length
Let me know what you think of this
Do you want the newsletter?
Do you want it monthly or quarterly or every 3 months?
Do you have a title suggestion in mind?
    This will by no means take the place of telephone calls. We will continue to call each other from time to time. Whatever the majority wants is the way we will go. So please cast your vote and let me know, ASAP.

Love your Sis,
Charlotte

    P.S. Come to find out, this newsletter has been Jessie's prayer since the sisters returned from our Atlanta trip. She had mentioned it in her letter to us. Somehow it did not penetrate to me at that time. She was praying again last week about it and behold! God finally got it through to me.

Jessie pours steaming water into her mug and eagerly pulls the teal-green stapled pages from the larger envelope. Propping up her feet, she begins reading again.

ISSUE NO. 1
MAY 26, 1996
OPENING WORD
by Charlotte

Praise God—this is it! Our FIRST "Family Newsletter"!! Everyone was really excited about doing this. I believe it's because we do it to honor our dear mother, ⎯ IDONA HOLLAND, ⎯ who loved her family so very much.

She was always doing anything possible to help and care for us. She was a very unselfish person, not just with her family, but with anyone who came in contact with her. She was the epitome of the name ⎯ "Good Neighbor." She was kind and neighborly to everyone on and around 526 E. Brackenridge Street. We never heard a bad word against her. And she and Daddy taught their children to respect the adults around us. If we forgot or "tried" them—the good ole "razor strap" was waiting for us. I'm sure we didn't like it at the time, but we can surely respect and appreciate that discipline now.

Mom loved her father and mother, sisters and brothers. She was always doing what she could to help them. And, most of all, she loved her God and Savior Jesus Christ. She was faithful to Him and to her church—Eliza Street Church of God, which later became McKee Street Church of God. No wonder she was named—"Mother of The Year" one year at the church.

While Mom was alive our family was very close. We gathered every year for her birthday, February 26th, and put on some sort of little play or skit for her. She giggled and repeated, ~~"Oh my goodness!" all through it. She thoroughly enjoyed having her children around her. Nothing would have pleased Mom more than to know that after she left this earth, her children stayed close and loved each other.

This newsletter is one way we can help accomplish that. It will keep us in touch with each other. This is a busy world we live in, and it's so easy to get wrapped up in our own little part of this world and unintentionally forget one another. But I believe Mother's spirit is still with us, and we do this to show our love for her and Daddy. And by all means we want to do what our Heavenly Father said: "Love one another as I have loved you."

BIBBA'S Corner

Hello All!

This is Barb, your Big Sister. Just to bring you all up-to-date; in a few months (November) I will be a real "honest-to-goodness" Senior Citizen.

Up to now, I have been denying that and claimed to be — 'Middle Age', (smile) However, I don't feel like a senior citizen. Isn't it amazing how time flies? Seems like only yesterday we were all playing "Tarzan" or "Beyond the Blue Horizon" in the back yard: climbing trees, playing ball, fighting, and getting spankings. (smile) Those were the days!! Well, enough of the nostalgia for now.

For those of you who don't know, I have three sons, two daughters, and 15 beautiful grandchildren. I am now retired from the Gas Co. after giving them 37 years of my life. I just got back from Tucson, Ariz., visiting and getting to know our brother Ken (Butchie) and Leonard (Twin #1) in California, a little better. These visits were long overdue.

God has truly blessed our family with long life, and all of us have been blessed with talents. I'll talk more about that and also my three months' stay out West in our next newsletter.

*** ** ***

MARSHA WETTER'S Corner

Hi! How is everyone doing? Just fine, I hope. We are all doing fine here in Fort Wayne. I am so glad to hear about the newsletter. I think it is a very good idea, also an excellent way to keep in touch. For my introduction, I am Marcia. Born Aug. 22. Divorced, and have 7 children.

I will be 63 on my next birthday and I "Thank the Lord" I am in good health, enabling me to still work everyday at Sears. Even though I am still working part-time with the grace of the Lord, I am still able to keep my home and pay the bills. I am trying to start a home business, like sewing or mail order or something to that effect, to help supplement. I will keep you posted if I can get this going. Meanwhile, let me know what the rest of you sisters and brothers are up to, in the newsletter.

Love you all!
Marci

*** ** ***

SHARKIE'S Corner

Hi All!

Can you believe it? —I was so engrossed in the "overall" newsletter, and concerned about everyone else getting their writing turned in, —I clean forgot that I also needed to write an article. (stop laughing!)

Anyhow, Jim and I just celebrated our 24th wedding anniversary April first. Remember that snow blizzard night when we all went bowling? Talk about "April Fools"!! Wow! (smile). Also, I just had my 61st birthday April tenth (Jim's was April second) — we took care of everything in one month! (smile) Like Barb said, I can hardly believe these many years have rolled past. But like Marci said, I thank the Lord for each and every one of them.

Five years ago, I took an early retirement from the University of Indianapolis (formerly known as Indiana Central College), where I worked in Printing for 32 years, all except the last five years, as supervisor/manager. For three months I had a "ball" running to the shopping malls daily, until Jim spoiled my fun and said I might as well get a part-time job out there. Wouldn't you know? – The first place I inquired (just to appease Jim) – said, Yes, we need help!! I had even turned the words around and asked, "You DON'T need help DO you?" Reluctantly, I worked as a clerk in a gourmet cookie shop. Then after two years I managed one of the shops downtown for a year. But it required too many hours, so I went back to part-time at the mall. This past January, I quit there and went to the Olive Garden restaurant as a seating hostess, on a part-time basis.

Since I have only one child to list, I figured I could write more about other things. Ritchie is living here in Indianapolis now. He left California about three years ago. He is 44 now and still unmarried. Will be thankful to God when that fellow really settles down and gets married. Hope it's not too late — I'm praying it is not.

So for the time-being, Jim and I have to be satisfied with our four-legged babies. They are all characters. One day I hope to write a book about all my wonderful dogs! Bye for now!!!

*** ** ***

JENNY'S Corner

Hi everyone, this is Cecelia. Just a few lines to bring you up-to-date on our family tree. We still live in Ft. Wayne, IN, but are looking toward moving to Denver Colorado, in the next couple or three years.

I am married to James and we have seven children. I also have older children by previous marriages. I have six step-children by James and we have eight grandchildren. I have twelve grandchildren from my older children.

Four of my children and nine of my grandchildren live here in Fort Wayne.

We have two foster children who are in the sixth grade.
We have another foster child who's in kindergarten.
We also have a foster child who's in Head Start.
We have two collies, Pepper and Lady.
Well that's about all for my family tree!

My husband still drives over the road for a major trucking company.
I am still on disability, but plan on returning to school to get a couple degrees.
We still love and serve the Lord with our whole heart, soul and mind.
I hope this letter gives you a little info about our household.
May God Bless You All in a very special way.

>Love you guys very much.
>Your Sister
>JENNY

*** ** ***

TWERP'S Corner

Hi Family,

I am so excited about our family newsletter. I hope everyone is as happy about it as I am. Charlotte said our first issue should be a re-introduction. Here goes!

My name is Jessie, or as Daddy use to call me, "Twet, Twop, Twerp." (smile) I am now married to a wonderful preacher named Thomas. We'll have been married 13 years this July 15.

These are my children and grandchildren:

1. My oldest child and daughter is age 36 (Ft. Wayne)
    - Her oldest child and daughter is age 18
    - Her next oldest is her son, age 16
    - Her third child is her son, age 8
    - Her fourth and baby is her daughter, age 7

2. My next oldest child is my daughter, age 33 (Ft. Wayne)
    - Her oldest child and daughter is age 18
    - Her second child is her son, age 16
    - Her third child is her daughter, age 12

3. My third child and daughter is age 32 (Indpls.)
4. Her oldest child and daughter is age 14

Those Holland Kids

>Her second child is her son, age 11
>Her third child is her son, age 4
>Her fourth child is her son, age 2
>Her fifth child is her son, age 11 mos.

5. My fourth child and daughter is age 25 (Indpls.)   (TWIN)
>Her oldest and only daughter is age 5
>Her only son is age 2

5. My fifth child is her twin, age 25 (Indpls.)   (TWIN)
>Her oldest and only son is age 4
>Her only daughter is age 2

6. My sixth child and daughter, age 20 (lives at home)
>Her only son is age 11 mos.

7. My seventh child and only son, age 18 (lives at home)

My occupation is homemaker. Plus I have several things I do at church. These duties are: Church Treasurer; Head of Music Dept.; Sunday School Superintendent; Sunday School Teacher for teenagers; and Teacher for Primaries. My hobbies are art, piano, and tennis. But most of all, I love to read. I'd rather read than watch TV.

Well, that's all for now. I have lots more to share with everyone. I love you all!

>Love,
>Your Sis,
>Jessie

*** ** ***

BUTCHIE'S Corner
Sorry, no info received. HOPEFULLY, next time.

*** ** ***

LUCY LOCKET'S Corner

HELLO *Sisters & Brothers!!*

Remember Me?

The Little Sweet one with the nice hair and gentle language? Of course you do. And as you would expect, I've grown up and have been transformed into the Sweet Big One — with gray hair and gentle language. Oh well, God is still able, isn't He?

Here goes —

I am Donna,

Medically disabled from the corporate (rat race) scene. Hobby: Private Individual Nutrition Counseling and Group Seminars.

Daughters:

My oldest daughter lives here in (Decatur, GA). She's married and has one daughter, age (5).

My next oldest daughter lives in (Jonesboro, GA), and is divorced with one daughter, age (14).

She is attending the American College of the Arts. She's working toward a double master's degree in Fashion Design and Marketing. She plans to transfer to a school in England for her 1997/1998 year and hopes to participate in work-study in France. She is currently in the process also of designing T-Shirts to market during "Freatnik" festivities.

My third oldest daughter lives in (Ft. Worth, TX). She's married and has one son, age (15), and one daughter age (2). She is in management for Krogers, where she has been employed for 14 years.

Those Holland Kids

My youngest daughter lives here in Atlanta. She's married and has a son, age (8 ½), one daughter, age (6), and another son, age (4). She is just getting settled after her relocation from Oklahoma City, and is planning to start a small catering business in several months.

We're all hyped-up for the Atlanta 1996 Summer Olympics to begin in July and August. It will be a very busy time for me (Lord willing). Hope I can make the deadline for our newsletter in July! Looking Forward,

So Long

*** ** ***

TWINS #1's Corner

Sorry, no info received. Hopefully, next time.

*** ** ***

TWINS #2's Corner

Sorry, no info received. Hopefully, next time.

*** ** ***

CLOSING WORD

Barb, ~ We Love the nostalgia! ~~~ let's have MORE!! Also, give us more detail on those "beautiful" grand-babies and children! Thanks for being inspired and coming up with our title: ~ "Those Holland Kids."And THANKS for the $5.00 donation toward the newsletter expense.

Marci ~~~ You really were excited about the newsletter. ~ Your article was FIRST in. Thanks for your speediness! But, ~ come on. ~ We know you're an "ole grandma" like the rest of us. Let us know how many grand-babies you have and how it breaks down per your children.

And — way-to-go! We will be praying for your home business.

Charlotte — Forgot to say that Ritchie is helping to carry on the Holland name. At this writing, he has said he is tired of the life he lived and has given his life back to the Lord! Praise God! I believe that "right" mate is coming his way soon.

Cecelia —— Your beautiful computer-typed copy looked too good for me to re-type, so I used it as was. Hope it's OK to indicate that four of your children are foster kids whom you and "Poogie" take as your own. What a good and noble thing to do: — giving needy children a better home life. But just don't over task yourself. ——We all want you well and in your "right mind." (smile) We all know what kids, kids, kids, can do to a person. (Well, everyone except ME — ha, ha, that's why I only had ONE!)

Jessie —— Hey girl, what precise info on your children and grandkids! I hope that you, also, don't over- task yourself. I was tired after just typing all the things you do in your church (and you didn't mention the things away from church).——I had to lay my head on the typewriter and take a nap before continuing. (smile) Hope I can get back to spending more time reading. These jobs I've had keep me so "hyped" up that when I sit to relax, — I go to sleep.

Donna —— Thanks for sharing what your girls are doing. The "Holland Talent" (which Daddy definitely had) runs all through our family. You sure are "cute" in those drawings! Looked just like you! (smile) Actually, thought they looked like me. (ha, ha).

But next time, make any drawings on a separate sheet of white, unlined paper and just indicate where they are to go, and I can paste them in on my typed sheet. But if at anytime (to all) your article comes "camera-ready," as Jenny's was, then make your drawing directly on your copy. Just be sure to use white, unlined 8 ½-x-11 paper. I like typing them — I'm just saying in case you decide to. And Donna, don't get too "energetic" and "athletic" while the Olympics are in your great city! It will seem EXTRA DULL after they are gone.

Kenny, Leonard and Linda — We hope after seeing and reading this first issue, you will not want to be left out of the next and the rest! Please try extra hard. — We WANT to hear from you. If you don't like to write, — send a taped message and I will type from it. Or you can call and I will record your message over the phone. Or, as a last resort, if you can catch a parrot and repeat to it and send him to me — that will work! (smile)
Seriously, let us HEAR from you.

*** ** ***

The cost of the newsletter is coming in right at just $6 (plus) for the size it is now. I can use regular size envelopes and the postage is normal. So if everyone wants to feel more "a part" of it, each could send $5 every two years. That means that each person is covering the cost of one newsletter, which is four times per year. I will pick up any slack or extras at all times. (Barb has paid hers.)

REMINDER: The next issue is due out August 26th. But since you all responded so well — (Marcia first, Jessie second, Donna third, Barbara fourth, Cecelia fifth, Charlotte sixth), you won't need to get your copy to me until AUGUST first (instead of July 26).
(or shortly after)

Almost forgot to Thank The Lord for inspiring me with the subtitle: "Then and Now." And a SPECIAL Thanks to our artistic Sis, Jessie, for "sprucing it up" REAL GOOD with the Beautiful Lettering!!!
                                           See you Next Time!
                                           Charlotte

chapter

Atlanta, Georgia
August 1996
Looking back; getting reacquainted

Donna sits listlessly on the front porch steps. The crisp morning breeze and quiet calm of the day would be comforting except for her melancholy mood. "I seriously dislike being the only sister living away from home. I get so lonely and homesick for the fun we have when we're together. During those times we are all usually trying to talk at the same time, Jenny is cracking jokes, or we have serious discussions about world affairs as they relate to Bible prophecy. That surprising and disturbing incident at our first sister-reunion was not a usual occurrence.

"I remember how it took me thirteen years after moving here to find a church I could call home. The incidents that led me to Christ Discipleship Ministries began when I became ill and then disabled. My job was super stressful and my marriage was even worse. I was working more than seventy hours a week as a life insurance agent. I had begun losing energy and getting nauseated after eating. As time progressed, my health worsened along with my marriage, which ultimately ended in divorce. I visited one doctor after another with no improvement while some of my health conditions turned chronic and others became acute. My weight dropped from 140 to 95 pounds.

"I can still vividly remember standing at the bottom of three flights of steps I had to climb for an insurance appointment. I just stood there, briefcase dangling at my side, staring up at that winding staircase. That was my last attempted appointment. I spent the next few years researching and engaging in natural remedies to build my strength and regain my health. I had only enough income to rent a room in a beautiful Christian lady's home. I stayed there well over a year.

"During my stay, another Christian lady, a minister, rented a room temporarily. As we came to know each other she told me the story of how and why she had sold her big, beautiful home that was in the same subdivision where we were living. While trimming a tree at their home, her husband had fallen to his death. The home was way too big for her to maintain alone so she put it up for sale.

"Discovering that I didn't attend church on a regular basis, she suggested I visit a church founded by a friend of hers, Christ Discipleship Ministries. I did make that visit and connected instantly with the Word being taught there.

"Shortly afterward, she moved away. By that time I had saved up enough money to buy a small condo. Now, was that Divine Connection or what?

"Looking back, I can see clearly how the Lord was with me through it all. Now I have changed my diet completely. I eat to live instead of living to eat. I have learned how to nurture my body with vitamins, minerals, and herbs. I have gained back the weight I need, have plenty of energy, and am closer to optimal health than I have ever been.

"And here is my mail truck with today's goodies." Donna races to the mailbox, waving at the driver as he maneuvers around the cul-de-sac. "Our second family newsletter! How timely!" She tears the large envelope open and finds canary-yellow pages; a welcome sight. Seated again on the steps, her heart instantly lifts as she begins reading.

ISSUE NO. 2
AUGUST 26, 1996

OPENING WORD
by Charlotte

Hello Everyone!

It certainly is GOOD to be typing our second family newsletter!! What a joy! What a blessing! What a privilege we have ----- to have all our sisters and brothers still alive and well on this Earth! There are a lot of families who sadly and unfortunately, cannot say this. But we can. Thank The Lord for keeping us all together up to this day!!

It has been a busy time for all of you this summer, I'm sure. But I'm so glad you took a little time to set aside for your family. Your sacrifice will make seven others a little happier ----- and you, too.

So sit back-----Relax-----and Enjoy your letters to each other!!!

BIBBA'S Corner

Hi Everybody!

I hope you all were as blessed as I was reading our first newsletter. Doesn't time fly? I'm really not prepared this time, but I'm doing the best I can. Since you last heard from me, I decided to take a part-time job at our church as bookkeeper and treasurer. Since we're using a computer, I enjoy the job more. I have taken a few short trips since May. Right now I'm in Pittsburgh for a few days, enjoying two of my kids and my grandchildren.

I went to the first service, 8 a.m., at Covenant Church of Pittsburgh this morning with them. Then, they went to the second service at 11:30 a.m., so I have the house to myself, relaxing and trying to think of something to say. (smile)

By the way, I left George at home. He pouted a little, but he's pretty good at letting me travel without him. Oh yes, I forgot to tell you what a pretty good guy George is. I do put him through a lot, though, because I'm sort of independent. I'll say that he has more patience with me than I have with him.

Do you remember at the first when I said I didn't know what to write about? I think I've taken up most of the space! (smile)

Love all of you and hope all of us brothers and sisters can get together before Jesus comes back!

Your Big Sis,
Barb

MARSHA WETTER'S Corner

Hi Sisters and Brothers!

Well, the time has come again to get in touch with each other. Update on my family: I would have written about them in my last letter, but I was not sure if you had enough space for all my children, grandchildren, and greats, (smile) --- so here goes.

My oldest daughter has 4 children and 8 grands.
My oldest son has 5 children and 9 grands.
My second oldest daughter has 3 children and 4 grands.

Those Holland Kids

My second oldest son has 4 children and no grands.
My third oldest son has 3 children and 2 grands.
My third oldest daughter has 1 child and no grands.
My fourth son, Darrin, has 1 child and no grands.

So you see why I didn't want to get started on this. I could go on and name all my grandchildren and my greats, but I'll leave that alone. I love every one of my grands and great-grands. They all call me Boo-Mama. That's because when Darrin was 8 or 9 years old, the teachers were always calling me to come to school about him. His nick-name was Boo, and every time I walked in the classroom, his classmates would say, "Here comes Boo's Mama," and everybody began to call me that. Here's a little bit of humor: Last year on my birthday, Roxanne called into the radio station, and had them announce, "Happy Birthday to Boo-Mama." I was so embarrassed. Speaking of birthdays, the 22nd has rolled around again. I'll be 63. They are coming too fast now! (smile)

I'm still working at Sears. I have not started my sewing business yet because I can't seem to find the time. My hobbies are my 30-gallon fish aquarium, my stereo system, and sewing for myself----clothes, slipcovers, and pillows ---- when I get the time to do it. I go bike-riding every Friday evening, with several of the children. Can you picture my clan riding down the street on bikes? ---- but it's fun!

So you see, I keep myself busy. I guess this is enough in this letter. I hope we hear from Linda and the brothers in the newsletter this time----- and remember ----- I love you all!

Marci

P.S. Charlotte,
---------I will be sending $5.00 to help you with the cost of the newsletter.

SHARKIE'S Corner

Hi Brothers & Sisters!

Here we are in the hot, muggy, midst of summer ---- ugh. This sort of weather, I don't like. All I want to do is run from one air-conditioned shopping mall to the next. (smile) Outdoor activities are not for me except early in the morning and when the sun is going down. My favorite of favorite seasons is coming up ----- Beautiful, cool, crisp, Fall! The trees will be showing off their gorgeous colors, ---- especially in Tennessee and the Carolinas, which ---- are my places to be at this time of year! Pray and hope one day Jim and I can live somewhere there.

Since our last newsletter, I quit working at Olive Garden restaurant the end of May. Thought I would enjoy being a "lady of leisure," but I'm experiencing an unsettling feeling. Can't really get into the things I thought I'd be doing. Kind of came to a standstill in my house decorating, don't read a lot, nor fix the nice, big delicious meals that Jim thought he would be getting -- (poor guy). Working was my good excuse ---- my "OUT" for not cooking all these years. But now, I have no excuse. When I do fix a meal, I feel pretty proud of myself. And then the next day I feel shocked and depressed when Jim says, --- "What are we having for dinner?" I say, --- "I just cooked yesterday! Don't tell me it's time to cook ---- AGAIN? Honey, can you get by with a TV dinner, or can we get Subway or something?" (smile) He is so sweet and goes along with it. I think, deep down, I want to go back to work! (only on a part-time basis) Then I can NOT COOK without feeling guilty. (smile)

On a little nostalgic note, I was talking with someone about musical talent. My thoughts went back to our house at 526 E. Brackenridge St. That was certainly a house where "music" was an important ingredient. What a joyous time we had when Daddy brought home our very first record player! Our dear Daddy--- Kenneth Holland --- dearly loved music! He could play any type of musical instrument, write and transpose the music, and even had a little band at one time. Mother even played the piano beautifully and sang. Daddy initiated many recitals for Barb and me at churches; --- she played the clarinet and I played the piano. I was always so nervous during those recitals. But we knew that we had to do well because Daddy was sitting out there critiquing us.

Each of us kids were required to take piano lessons as soon as we could say our ABC's. I always remember the day Daddy took my hand and led me to the "Fort Wayne College of Music" -- (not a college really) for my first piano lesson. I think Barbara and Marcia were already enrolled playing the xylophone.. (hope I spelled it correctly --can't find my dictionary). We kids would put on Talent Shows for Mom and Daddy, shows taken from a radio program called "Major Bows". They would sit and be the judges while each one of us did our "little thing" ---- played piano or sang a song or such. Out of these sessions, Daddy must have sensed that I had a voice that could be developed. He asked if I wanted to take voice lessons. Of course, I was so excited! But the extra money never came for those lessons. And whatever was there in me for singing never came forth. I think how proud Daddy would be if he could hear his son, Kenny Jr. and his daughters sing. He'd also be delighted to hear his daughters, Jessie and Donna play the piano. We all may not be involved directly in music now, but we all appreciate and love music.

Daddy would be proud of each and every one of his children for just having good professions, (since he was such an intellectual) --- like Linda's writing ability, Leonard's engineer's mind, Marcia's sewing talents, Donna's ability to be an entrepreneur in business, Barbara's and my many years in the business world. Mom was certainly proud of her children. She spoke of it many times with her beautiful smile on her face. She'd ---- say: "Kenny would really be proud of you children."

I will end on that word.

Love, your sis,
Charlotte

JENNY'S Corner

Hey Gang!

What's up? Good way to start a letter, huh? With two questions. Well you should know by now who this is from. Nothin' much has changed; ----- my life is just as dull as ever.

One of my foster children is no longer with me, so I just have four children. And by the time school starts, another one will probably be adopted out.

I am still taking voice and piano lessons. ---- I'll be a "Star" yet! (smile)

They are still working on our new addition to the house. For those of you who haven't heard about it, let me fill you in. We are adding a master bedroom with a full bath and walk-in closet. Also a dining room with an area for a sofa, a couple of chairs and cocktail and end tables, with a sliding door that leads out to the patio. Also, we removed the old door that was in the breeze-way and put a sliding door there. We are turning the garage into a family room. They will remove my old window out of the living room and replace it with a bay window. New carpet will be laid in the living room and on the stairs, and down the upstairs hallway. I'm going to lay tile down in the upstairs bathroom, too, and redecorate it myself. They are putting in central air, also. Hopefully, everything will be done by the end of August. We concreted the whole patio area and also along the side of the garage to the driveway. Next year, ---- if the Good Lord says the same, ---- we are going to put up a 2 ½ - car garage in the back of the house. This really turned out to be a bigger project than I thought it would be.

The Lord has really blessed us beyond measure! We have a wedding to go to on the tenth of August. I'm supposed to sing "Wind Beneath My Wings." Keep me in your prayers.

Let's remember all of our unsaved children and relatives in our prayers. Pray that they will see their need to repent and be saved before it is everlasting too late.

May God Bless and Keep each and every one of you in perfect health. And may you be prosperous in ALL things.

> Love all of you,
> Your sister,
> Jenny

TWERP'S Corner

Hi again Family!!!

It's that time again. I've been looking forward to this day. I enjoyed our first newsletter so much. It brought tears to my eyes. I've read it several times now. Yes, I know, little emotional Jessie. (smile)

I am so proud of all my sisters and brothers. As a matter of fact, I think I have the GRANDEST family in the world! I couldn't wait to call Charlotte after I read the newsletter. She was at work, so I blurted out my praises for an outstanding job to her answering machine.

Tom and I just celebrated our 13th Wedding Anniversary on July the 15th. We were able to go to the Niagara Falls. WHOOPEE-E!! Those falls are breathtaking. I bought cards for everyone, but they were so beautiful I decided to keep them.

No, seriously. I'm not one for sending cards. (Did I hear you all say, "We know!"?) It's no problem getting the cards. It's just finding stamps and a mailbox in a strange city. But I was thinking about you all. Honest to goodness!

Rhonda, my eldest has finished two years of law school. She's determined to be a criminal lawyer. She went as far as she could in Ft. Wayne. She's looking at finishing in Florida or Atlanta. I'm so proud of her. She has a lot of determination as a single mother.

I didn't mention that Joey, my only boy, has carried on his mom's artistic talents. He astounded everyone with his drawing when he was very young. I accused him of copying until I saw it with my own eyes. He's into airbrushing. He has a neat little business designing T-shirts, pants, jackets, and whatever. He's very good. He also plays piano and keyboard. He plays for our church. I taught him beginner piano, then he took off and left me in his dust. He plays by ear.

I can't tell you about all my kids in this issue but hope I'll be able to send pictures of them and all my grandchildren soon. We had pictures taken at a little reunion in March.

Well, family, I'm going to close for now. Me and this word processor don't get along too well. I'm just learning. (smile) It's taking far longer than I thought. And also, I'm sleepy. I woke up around 3 this morning. Since I couldn't go back to sleep I figured this would be a good time to write. So long, for now. I love you all!

Jessie Mae

P.S. Donna, I'll be calling you after the Olympics when you're rested. My eyes are glued to the TV. It's exciting! That opening was awesome. I know Atlanta is proud.

KENNY, KENNY, KENNY,... WHERE IS MY TAPE?

BUTCHIE'S Corner

No Info Received. ------ Come on, No. 1 Son. --- let us hear about your exciting singing career!

LUCY LOCKET'S Corner

Hi Ya All

It's time again. It seems like just yesterday since our last newsletter. I'll start out by praising The Lord my God for all He's done and what He is doing and Who He Is!!!

Now, I'll bring you up-to-date on what's happening here in Atlanta.

No. 1. The Olympics

I didn't rent the house, which worked out good for me because I was too involved in another project that would have caused a conflict. Even so, the Olympics have created many problems for Atlanta business owners. Most in the downtown area have closed their doors for the entire three-week period in anticipation of traffic jams; others are complaining about the 70% decrease in their business. Atlanta customers are staying home for fear of being trampled by Olympic ticket-holders. So here's the whole story.

'Twas the night before Olympics,
When all through the town
All the people are excited
and running around;
The Shop owners were standing
by their windows with care, in hopes that the Big Spenders
soon would be there;
The waitresses were nestled, all snug in their beds, while visions
of Dollar Signs danced in their heads;
Now in restaurants, now in Malls
now in Markets and Fairs!
They'll be dining and shopping
for all sorts of Wares!
Atlantans and family and I and my cap
Had just settled in for a 3-week nap, ------
When out in the town, there arose such a clatter,
I sprang from my bed to see what was the matter.
Away to the window, I flew like a flash,
tore open the shutter and threw up the sash.
When what to my wondering eyes should appear,
but a Host of Angry Venders and Waitresses
with a Terrible Sneer.

Those Holland Kids

With So Many frustrated faces and
spirits so glum,
I knew in a moment that the Crowds had Not come.
No Dining, no Shopping, no Tipping TODAY!
"What Happened?"
The Stupid Media!!
They Frightened The Crowds Away!!

True Story (Smile)
****

(just a note, I dreamed up this poem myself,
maybe I should start writing poetry)

****

No. 2. The Family Portrait Project

Most of you know that I have a dedicated portion of wall space for the display of family portraits. I have since decided to convert the bonus room off of the downstairs den into a portrait room and lounge, God willing; I will use all four walls for family portraits. I have everyone's photograph except Cecelia, Marcia, and Leonard. I'm in the process of enlarging Barb's, Linda's and Kenny's to 8-x-10. Jessie's, Charlotte's, Mom's, Daddy's, and Granddaddy's are all beautifully framed and ready to hang.

This has been so much fun for me, ---- even somewhat therapeutic. (smile). So please Cecelia, Marcia, and Leonard, send me your photos ---- any size will do. If the best you can do is a family portrait, I'll take it -----"PRONTO."

Well, So Long for Now!
Donna

TWIN NO. 1's Corner

No Info Received. ----- Leonard, what's happening in Beautiful Cal - i - forn - i - a??

TWIN NO. 2's Corner

No Info Received. ----- Linda, Linda, Linda, we all KNOW how good you can write ---- No Excuse!

CLOSING WORD

Good Job Everyone!

You see ---- you could do it. Several said, prior to the deadline: ----- "I don't know what to write about." Let's face it. Everyone does not have the ability to put their thoughts down on paper and write "mini books" like some of us. That's understandable. But please don't let this wonderful thing we have cause you to be "stressed-out." This is supposed to be ------ FUN!! Don't make it a chore. Don't think of it as writing an article for the newspaper in your city.

A Few Suggestions:
When you receive the "Reminder Post Card," tape it up where you'll be sure to see it every day. Start thinking back over the past 2 1/2 months. Jot down the highlights of events that happened to you and your family, as you think of them. (Or you could have already jotted down these events during the 2 1/2 months, as they happened.) Don't do like I have been guilty of doing: --- jot things down on any piece of paper, and then can't find the piece of paper. Have a special little notebook.

Find a time when you can have your private "quiet time" or reflection. Read over the last issue to remind yourself of something you were supposed to include or make a comment about, in the upcoming issue. Then ask The Lord to open up your memory. Think back on our wonderful years as "Those Holland Kids on Brackenridge Street." All you need is One incident to remember. No need to write a book about it ---- (like I did) (smile). ---- Just tell something about it, best you can. Maybe someone else will remember some more about that event and will share it the next time. In any case, just don't let this make you feel like you're back in school having to write an ESSAY---- That will really turn you OFF!

Again, I send forth a plea to Ken, Linda and Leonard ---- you ARE a part of our family, ---- and you CAN'T change that, ever. So why not make up your minds to join in the Fun? One day in the future, if Jesus tarries, you won't want to look back with regrets of what could have been. Time is flying past so very fast! So if you absolutely don't like to write, why not send a taped message? You can purchase a pack of cheap 30-minute tapes. After you have sent all three to me, I will mail them back to you to re-use over again. You can't beat that offer!

Barb ----That proves it, we just can't get away from the work world, can we? But it's better since you are now working in the church.
You were really relaxed up there in Pittsburgh ---- all alone ---missing your "sweetie," George. After you talked about him, ---- you must have gone right off to sleep (zzzz zzzz) ----- and dreamed sweet dreams of being back in his arms. (smile)

Marci ...Or should I say, "Boo-Mama"! You see how informative this newsletter is? We never heard that before! Thanks for the run-down on your children and grands. Again, I'm shocked ---- didn't know I had so many grand and great nieces and nephews! (wow!) Your letter was really hilarious!!

CeCe... Knew about your voice lessons, but didn't know piano was in there also. Go on girl ---- not only are you going to be another "Dino," but also another "Mahalia Jackson"! That's great! I should follow after you. We won't recognize your house when we come to Ft. Wayne. Talk about a COMPLETE face-lift! It sounds beautiful! Can't wait to see it! You may not be turning cartwheels ----but your life sounds anything but ----- dull!

Jess... You did Great on that Word Processor! Glad I didn't have to trace around all those cute little faces. But really, that is good artwork, ---- really clever! Tell Rhonda that it sure will be good to have a "Marsha Clark" in the family! And tell Joey (we can't say "little Joey" any longer); we are proud of him! THANKS for the $5 on newsletter postage.

Donna... That's really a shame that the wonderful Olympics brought such disappointment to so many. That whole story was really neat! The Portrait room sounds wonderful! Can't wait to see it. PLEASE Cecelia, Leonard and Marcia ---- get your picture to her right away!! Don't forget! It's so easy to plan to do it and forget. Write a note to yourself and put it up where visible. That's a lot of work going into "our family portrait display" --- a Labor of Love --- THANKS, Donna!

Our next newsletter will go out November 26th. Your letters will be due anytime before the third week. I will send out reminders on the first and you'll have a couple weeks to get them in. You're doing good sending them in. This time Jessie Mae was first in, Donna Lucille second, Barbara Louise third, and Cecelia Jennette and Marcia Jean were tied fourth.

Pray we all have a Wonderful, Happy, Healthy, Beautiful Fall!

       Bye for Now.
       Charlotte

chapter

5

November 1996
What! an early end to our newsletter?

"November in Indianapolis is always so lovely," Charlotte muses as she surveys the defined patches on the lawn created by the freshly-fallen snow. She has almost a full view of the landscape through the large picture window. Her four-footed babies are each in their places of comfort next to the sofa close to her feet. "I love my doggies, even though they are each a real piece of work." `

Charlotte turns her attention back to the steel-gray stapled pages in her hands. "Speaking of a piece of work, these sister-gals of mine are getting on my last nerve. We are only on our third issue and everybody is starting to fizzle out. I hope I'm not being too hard on them in my opening remarks, and as for those still refusing to participate, shame, shame!"

Settling back carefully so as not to disturb her four sleeping beauties, she continues, "I'll reread this entire third issue one more time before I mail each one a copy." She begins her critique.

Those HOLLAND Kids THEN and NOW
"Bibba" "Marsha Wetter" "Sharkie" "Jenny" "Jwet" "Butchie" "Lucy Locket" "Twins" "BARBARA" "MARCIA" "CHARLOTTE" "CECELIA" "JESSIE" "KENNETH" "DONNA" "LEONARD" "LINDA"

ISSUE NO. 3
NOVEMBER 26, 1996

OPENING WORD
by Charlotte

Hi Everyone!

Well, this Number 3 ----- You would think it was 30, the way some seemed to be "fizzing out". We are just getting started good, so don't get burned out so soon. Come on, ---- this is what we ALL wanted. This is not MY thing. I send out the reminder cards because I realize how easy it is in our busy world to forget what month the newsletter is due. But after I take time to do that, then, I expect everyone to be responsible to put that card where you will see it daily and then RESPOND in a relatively decent time. Again, I want to emphasize that this should NOT be taken as a chore; ---- it's supposed to BE FUN!!!

I hear things like, "I don't know what to say." You don't have to be an author or experienced writer. Just imagine that you're talking on the phone. Just say what you've have been doing the last three months. It doesn't have to be exciting and ---- exotic. We are not in a contest to see who has done the most. We just want to know how you and your family are. If you have been down, then ---- tell us you have been down and ask us to pray for you. If nothing interesting has happened in your life lately, then just tell us. It boils down to this ---- WE JUST WANT TO HEAR FROM EACH OTHER!!

You have a few SURPRISES in this issue. ---- I'm sure you will be PLEASED!

Charlotte smiles with satisfaction. "Hey, I think it's gonna be okay. I have faith that we all will be revitalized and enthusiastic about our future newsletters. After all, we did agree it was the Lord who gave us the idea and the inspiration." She lets out a little chuckle and continues reading, now concentrating on Barbara's article.

BIBBA'S Corner

Hi Sisters & Brothers!

Well, here I am again at the last minute trying to get this note written before we reach Indianapolis. It's Sunday A.M. and we (Charlotte, Marcie and myself) just left Decatur, Illinois, where we were blessed with an anointed two-day "spiritual banquet." This Joyce Meyer seminar was one of the Best. The Word of The Lord sure blessed me and related to exactly what I've been going through for the last three months. I really Thank God for this time of spiritual refreshing whenever life's pressures get to us. God has a way for us to turn aside and reflect on His Grace and Mercy and to help us take one more spiritual step upward. GOD IS SO GOOD!!!

Linda, it was so nice hearing from you the other day, and it was a pleasant surprise hearing your voice and to know that you and your children are doing well.

Leonard, it would be nice if you would give any of us a call, or better yet, participate in our newsletter and let us know how you and your family are doing. WE LOVE YOU.

Kenny, Lord willing, I'll be seeing you shortly. But why don't you treat the rest of your sisters and brothers with a hello and a few lines. WE ALL LOVE YOU.

Well, "Kids," it's about time for me and George to migrate with the birds (smile) to Arizona in about three weeks. I can hardly wait! Well, this is it for now ---- I'm sure I'll have more to report next time.

Your Big Sis,
Barb

MARSHA WETTER'S Corner:

Hi Everyone!

I hope to read that everyone is feeling good and good things are working in your lives. I hope that this time I will hear from Linda. She is still our baby sister and I love her too. I don't expect to hear from the brothers, but I hope they are doing fine also. Donna, I was sorry to hear about your marriage ending. I am sure you did everything you could to save it. And knowing you, you will not let it get you down.

I want everyone to know that Brackenridge Street neighborhood no longer exists, only in our hearts and memory. I went past there one day this week and the only house sitting on the whole block was the house the Garfields stayed in. The house is now some kind of project office. They fixed it up and it looks nice. The neighborhood looks different because all houses on both sides of the street are gone. I hope most of us have a picture of our house at 526 E. Brackenridge Street.

Well, believe it or not, I am writing this letter from Decatur, Illinois. I am here with Barbara and Charlotte at the Holiday Inn. We are here for two days to hear the ministry of Joyce Meyer. She is a dynamic speaker, and I am enjoying every session we have attended so far.

It is getting cold now and everyone is getting ready to settle down at home for a cold and nasty winter, ---- all except Barbara. I hear she is going to desert us and move to Tucson for six months. But when it gets warm again, she will come back home. There ought to be a law against people doing that sort of thing. (smile) But since it is not, ---- I am happy for her! I only wish I could do the same thing!

Well, maybe some day I'll be able to.

Jessie, as if you aren't smart enough already! I hear you are taking classes on getting smarter and making money as well. Good Luck on your Income Tax Preparation Course!

The Holidays are coming up before our next newsletter, ----- so I am wishing everyone a Nice Thanksgiving, a very Merry Christmas, and a Happy New Year!!! Until next time, ----- I Love You All! Thank you Barbara and Charlotte for a nice time in Decatur!

Marci

SHARKIE'S Corner

Hey Gang!

What a joy to be involved in another Family Newsletter! I really mean it. I get excited typing and reading each letter! It really makes me feel closer to each of you. If a lot of families did this, they would be amazed what it would do for their relationships.

The last three months have been busy, busy for me. I go to Drug Stores, etc., and straighten up the Sunglasses & Reader Glasses racks. People sure do get them all out of their proper places. Then according to their needs, I write orders for more and write credits for damages. It's fun in a way. And I am my own boss as to what day or days I go out, and how many stores I service that day. The only requirement is to service them monthly, and a few are serviced every two weeks. I got curious and counted the stores in my book and discovered there were 74. ---- I said, ---- "No wonder I'm so tired." My District Manager is a real neat guy (lives in Kentucky). So, I told him I didn't want that many stores. ---- (I'm supposed to be retired!)

I need and want to spend more time with my dear hubby, Jim, my big baby, "Sheba" & my little baby, "Little Ricky," and our new, darling, beautiful little Pomeranian doggie. He is small, but acts like a TIGER who will "eat you up" when someone comes in the house. ---- (Ask Jessie, Marcia and Barb.) But then after I introduce him to them, ----- they can't get rid of him! He is a "mess." Sheba is so BIG and he is so "little," ---- you should see them trying to play together.

Please remember Ritchie in your prayers. He is up and doing relatively good when he gets away from that crazy girl friend he goes with. But when they get back together, ----- he goes way down again. He really needs help! I have given up trying to run to his rescue each time, since I see it does not really help matters. It's like he is going around in circles and has me going around with him. I have decided to really turn it over to The Lord, who is the ONLY ONE who can help Ritchie get up and out FOR GOOD!

I do believe prayer ---- especially prayer out of agreement ---- works! Let's AGREE IN PRAYER, ----- not only for Ritchie, but for all our family needs, ---- and EXPECT God to move. I believe we have set Sundays as the Day we all will Pray ---- for our Family. Be sure to include that you are AGREEING IN PRAYER with the others. Remember, Jesus said, "If TWO shall AGREE as touching anything that they shall ASK, it SHALL be DONE for them of my FATHER which is in Heaven." ------ Wow! What a Promise! (Matthew 18:19)

Barb, Marcia and I went to Decatur, Illinois, to two Beautiful, Wonderful, Glorious, Marvelous, days of seminars!! Oh, how Anointed were those meetings! And the music of Praise & Worship was absolutely Out of This World!! Wish you ALL could have been there! When they sang a couple old hymns that I remembered us singing back in church in Ft. Wayne when Mom, Granddaddy and Grandma were there ---- like Leaning, Leaning on the Everlasting Arms. I had my eyes closed, and it felt like I was dancing in the Arms of Jesus! I kid you not. I used to LOVE to dance, but had not since being Saved. So when I was sort of moving slightly to the music, with my arms up; ------- it felt SO GOOD to be dancing with My Saviour Jesus!!!

Well, I had better cut this off now. See you Next Time!

Love
Charlotte

JENNY'S Corner
No letter received.

*** * ***

TWERP'S Corner

I just finished reading the August newsletter. Oh my, it gets gooder and gooder! Why am I just now reading it? It's not that I was disinterested. It seems my letter took the long way home ---- by way of Ft. Wayne. I'll let Charlotte expound on it. But seriously, I was feeling just like a little kid waiting on a wonderful surprise package, and when it got delayed, I was getting frantic! ----

Those Holland Kids

- Oh, I won't keep you in suspense. Someone, (won't say who), was supposed to drop it off to me, but instead gave it a little pleasure trip to Ft. Wayne. (smile) It was well worth the wait! I got teary-eyed, again, reading about Mom and Daddy. "Oh, here I go again!" Oh you guys, I won't cry! I just love our family so much and it's true, God has Blessed us. For that I Praise Him!

It is now Nov. 11th and I'm just now getting back to this letter. I know ---- shame, shame! I've been so busy, it doesn't make any sense. Guess what I went and did? In my "old age," I have the audacity to take a tax class. Boy, is my little brain getting a workout!! (Wow!) I didn't realize there was so much involved with taxes: Depreciation, Amortization, IRA, and on and on and on. I feel like a kid in first grade. But The Lord hears and honors prayers. I've been getting A's & B's on all my tests and quizzes. I guess there's hope!

Enough about today. We were supposed to write something about the "old days." My mind goes back to Brackenridge Street to two incidents that stick in my mind. The first has to do with a baby. I thought it was Donna. I remember Mom in a big bed. (I thought it was Grandma's house, but someone said Donna wasn't born at Grandma's). But I remember Daddy buying me some new shoes and picking me up so Mom could see them. I was real small. Could that have been Kenny since we are two years apart? I remember it was a little pale baby.

Second, I remember when all of us kids were peeking in the window of our next-door neighbor, spying on her with her boyfriend. She came and told Daddy. Daddy waited all day, saying nothing. Everyone was scared to death. Then he called us all into the kitchen. Starting with the oldest, he took us upstairs one-by-one. We could hear the hollering going on upstairs. We were trembling, waiting on our turn.

Finally, Daddy got to me; I was the youngest. He must have taken one look at my skinny, trembling legs and took pity on me, because I didn't get a whipping. Boy! Was I happy! I was in on it, although someone had to hold me up to see in the window. To this day, I don't even remember what I saw. (smile)

Those were happy days and I Thank God for the memories. So long for now, family. I Love You All!

Love,
Jessie

*** * ***

BUTCHIE'S Corner
No letter received.

LUCY LOCKETT'S Corner

My! My! How time flies!! I can't believe it's time again, but I've been looking forward and have been making myself notes to remember things to say. Problem is, I can't put my hands on them or the last newsletter to refer to. So can't really respond to questions or requests. Sorry.

AND NOW THE WEATHER REPORT..
It has been 70–75 degrees up until today, Fri. 11/8.
It's starting to get "Cold" --- 60 degrees (smile).

This was all very sudden: My house is up for sale, as of 1 1/2 weeks ago. Two offers came in this week and I accepted the better offer. I'm praying that it all goes through OK. Someone I know advised me to buy a St. Joseph statue from the Catholic Bookstore and bury it face down in the front yard, because St. Joseph is supposed to be the Saint of Real Estate. Well, her solution sounded somewhat pagan to me and I chose to trust in the God of the Whole Earth, ---- "Lord Jesus." I went back to that girl after the house sold and told her my testimony.

I do remember that we're supposed to remember about our childhood years on Brackenridge. The times I recall are when Jessie and I tested our musical talents by choreographing a duet that we danced to. We put on the record Goofus on that old phonograph and we tapped out our little twosome to the rhythm of...

Don't read notes, but I play everything by ear,
I made a tune by the sounds that I used to hear.
Folks used to say (tap)!
As I used to play (tap)!

Sounds a little Goofus to me (tap, tap)!

That's all the lyrics I can remember, but we danced for hours and nobody could have convinced us that we weren't off to "vaudeville." I used to know more of the lyrics so if anybody remembers more of the verses, put them in the next newsletter. I'll be looking forward!!

I also remember sneaking up behind the sofa where Charlotte was sitting and courting a beau --- or was it Barbara? ---- Don't remember. But I surprised them when I threw a broken doll's head onto his lap as I started singing the old song, "I ---------- Ain't Got No Bo-------dy -------, and no body cares for me."----."

I think you told Mom on me, but I don't remember getting a spanking, ----- perhaps Mom recognized my musical talents and bypassed the punishment.

The picture that comes to mind most often is opening the front door to get the milk left by the milkman. It was always sooooo cold, and usually covered with snow, and so good. It tasted almost as good as that white wedding cake Daddy would dish out to us by the handfuls as we lined up next to each other sitting on the floor. Yum, Yum! Cake just doesn't taste good like that any more, does it?

Well, I must cut this short for now; I have to prepare for a Nutritional Seminar (rather, a one-hour presentation). It will be next week for the weight-loss group "Tops, Inc." a national support chain. My topic is "Simple Tips To Live By." I've lost a little weight lately, so hope they can see me as I speak to them. --

Oh well, life is fun, isn't it? I'm really excited about this one. I really enjoy public speaking. I always make it fun and tell lots of little jokes along with what I believe is Great Info!

Until Next Time... So Long!
    Donna

*** * ***

TWIN LEONARD'S Corner
No letter received.

TWIN LINDA: I LOVE AND THANK EACH OF YOU WHO ENCOURAGED AND HEPED ME, I LOVE YOU ALL VERY MUCH! My children are all doing fine. My grandchildren are all fine, as well. Thank God!
THANK GOD FOR HIS WISDOM AND GOODNESS!
A THOUGHT FROM THE WORD! ----

Ecclesiastes 10:19 "A Feast Is Made For Laughter, And Wine Maketh Merry, But Money Answereth All Things." Growing up in a church that put the FEAR of MONEY in me, I had to wrestle with Poverty all of my life. My point is, don't Love Money, don't make it your Rose Picture god, but do know that it is GOOD. It is a necessary tool to live and do God's will/works. Don't FEAR IT!

THE "INNER PAUPER" ALWAYS COME UP WITH :
EXCUSES
INDECISIONS
CATASTROPHIC EXPECTATIONS
ALWAYS MOTIVATED BY THE FEAR OF:
FAILURE
SUCCESS
NEVER MAKING IT
LOSING IT
FEAR CAUSES US TO CLOSE OUR MINDS IN TIGHT
LITTLE BALLS
CONFIDENCE ALLOWS US TO OPEN OUR MINDS WIDE
LETTING FRESH IDEAS IN!

Those Holland Kids

God is truly blessing me. I thank Him for all my experiences and for every person in my family. I love you all and wish you all a Happy Thanksgiving Day and hope you're thankful for what He is doing, as well as, not doing in your life at this time! He loves you more than you or anyone else could ever love you!

I'm not trying to preach. I simply felt led to write what was on my heart, because I'm thinking that someone in our family really needed to hear it. Maybe one of my children, your children, our cousins, uncles, or aunts... whoever. I had to write it!

Charlotte, you're doing a great job, keep up the Great Work! I'm very proud of you!

Love Linda (Twin)
Always!

CLOSING WORD

Once again, we have completed another "Family Newsletter." In fact, this is the LAST one for this year. We ended up the year with a few ---- surprises. As I mentioned in the Opening Word. "No. 1":----We are happy to have Baby Sis, Linda in this issue. Not only was it a joy to receive her letter, ---- which was first, ----- I might add, but also a phone call. She called Leonard and his wife and we had a (three-way conversation) and it was sure good to talk with them. The "No. 2" surprise is that they SAID they would send a letter, but guess something happened. Also, "No.3," Jessie said that Kenny and Wife SAID they would be sending a letter this time, but didn't quite make it. At least we are getting WARMER! But then, "No. 4," we lost Cecelia's letter this time. We have something to look forward to for the New Year ----- 100% Participation! Right?

We want to Thank Linda for the beautiful copy and message she sent in from her computer. Glad to hear all your children are fine, Linda. Also, the back page "Thanksgiving Greeting" was from her. Thanks, also, Linda, for your monetary contribution to the newsletter.

We wish Barb and George Godspeed and pray the Angels are encamped around them as they journey to (and from) Tucson for the winter. I agree with you Marci, ---- It must be NICE to be able to do this!
Marci, ---- thanks for giving us that report on Brackenridge Street. HOW SAD! I know when I see it, I will surely CRY!! If anyone does have a photo

of our house, ----- please make copies to share with us all.

Jessie, we won't use that Carrier Service again. It wasn't UPS, ------ but it was BLC. (smile) Do we need to spell it out, Barb? And I do remember the whipping Daddy gave us that you mentioned. Good thing you escaped it. It either pays to be "little", or "knowing how to let those legs tremble"! But I'm quite sure ALL OUR legs were trembling, ----- so it had to be because you were the littlest!

OK, Donna, ----- you've proved to us that you are AN ARTIST! Don't remember that being me on the couch with a boyfriend ---- must have been Barbara. But I do remember you and Jessie ALWAYS hugged up together TRYING to dance. In fact, we were beginning to think you were Siamese Twins, joined at the hips or head! I remember the song, Goofus, but don't remember any more verses. That was a cute song.

Hope you enjoy the surprise "No.5" ------ the enclosed Tape! I'm so glad I found it and was able to share it with you all.

Adding my wish for a Happy Thanksgiving, --- a Blessed & Merry Christmas, and a Prosperous, Healthy, & Joyous NEW YEAR!

Next issue will be "February, 1997!" ---- Mother's Birthday Anniversary! Try to include a memory about her SPECIFICALLY.

*** * ***

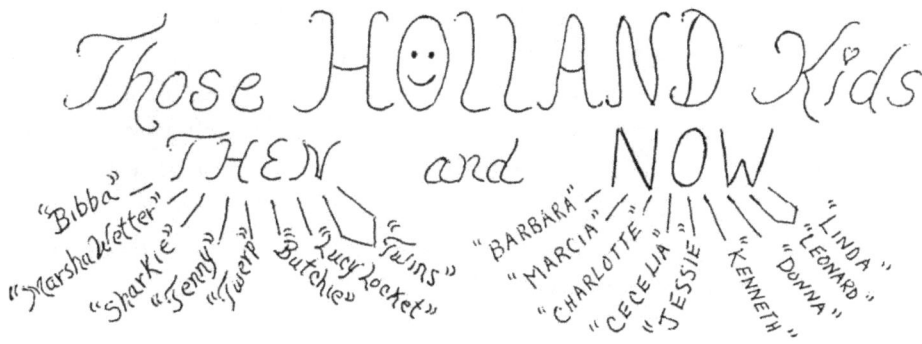

Those Holland Kids

ISSUE NO. 3
NOVEMBER, 1996
JENNY'S Corner

Hello Again,

I'm really running late this time. I've had so much going on until some times I don't know who I am. Well how's the gang doing? I hope the Lord is Blessing everyone.

Not much to tell this time. The addition is completed, but I still have curtains to put up, and I still haven't gotten my dining room furniture yet.

I have only four foster children, now, and the adoption on the three should be done by the end of the year. I have a new grandchild who is 3 months old! That's James III's son. I babysit during the week for him. He is a cutie!

We are all doing fine. I hope I have some juicy stuff to tell you about next time. God Bless all of you and hope to hear from you soon.

Love,
Your Sis,
Jenny

EDITOR'S Note:
by Charlotte

Well, CeCe, -----it's "Better Late Than Never!" I had given up on you, but so glad that you came through!! Your letter came on Wednesday (day before Thanksgiving), after I had completed the newsletter Tuesday night and had Jim go with me to run it off. Wanted to have it all packaged up so that Jessie could take the Ft. Wayne ones with her on Thursday. I had a full day on my job Wednesday, so didn't want to put every thing off until then. Can't wait to see your home. ---- I know it must be BEAUTIFUL! Also, can't wait to see this NEW little addition to the family!! Hey, you all, ---- what do you suppose this "juicy stuff" is that she is going to tell us next time? Let's see: ---- Maybe she and Poogie ran off to that seminar last week and had a "torrid" love renewal, ---- and she is ----- PREGNANT!!!! (wow!) I can hardly WAIT!!! (smile)

A Time To
Be Thankful
For Those
HOLLAND
KIDS!

Those Holland Kids

Laughing out loud, Charlotte lays the colorful pages aside. Little Rickie sits up watching her. Rambo and Sheba stretch and yawn. "Now look what I've done," she scolds herself jokingly. "I've just put an end to my quiet time." Little Rickie leaps up onto her lap while Rambo and Sheba get up on all fours. Not to be forgotten, Mr. French stretches his long frame, preparing to join the pack.

chapter

6

February 1997
Remembering Mama

Marcia pulls the stack of mail from the mailbox and flips through it on her way to her front door. She lets herself in and is excited to find a large envelope amongst the mound of letters and junk mail. "Oh, here's our newsletter! What a welcome surprise," she says aloud.

She hangs up her coat and almost simultaneously kicks off her shoes. "My job this week has been unusually stressful. Today was the worst I've experienced in a while. I remember saying to myself at lunchtime, 'Lord, I need an attitude check up from the neck up.' So this newsletter issue is exactly what the doctor ordered."

After rushing through her after-work routine, Marcia settles onto the velvety comforter and turns on the lamp next to her bed. She has adjusted the space heater at the other end of the room but the huge matching pillows still feel too cool so she reaches for the soft fleece blanket at the foot of the bed. Comfortable at last, she retrieves the soft purple stapled pages from the envelope and begins reading.

ISSUE NO. 4
FEBRUARY 26, 1997

OPENING WORD
by **Charlotte**

Hi Family!

What a Wonderful newsletter we are going to have this time! I have not read any of the articles at this time, but I'm anticipating them all to be GREAT!

Those Holland Kids

This issue is in memory of our precious dear Mother, ------ Idona Holland. ------ being that her birth date was February 26th. And as you all remember, we use to really celebrate at those times! That was the "one" day of the year we all got together (if at all possible) in Ft. Wayne and did something "SPECIAL" for Mom. As I recall, it was usually some sort of skit or such. Then once we gave her a big scrap-like book with letters from each sister/brother, with each of their children writing something to Grandmother, also. There was a photo of each family with their greetings. Barb should still have that book. Someday I would like to read it through again.

WE LOVE YOU MOM!!

Since you can't be here with us, ------- we are glad you are with --------- JESUS!!!

BIBBA'S Corner

Hello All!

Well, we (George and I) are pretty well settled here in Tucson. We have our apartment furnished as best we can. We may even spend the summer out here with the exception of a couple of weeks to go get our car. (I'm sick and tired of driving that big van.)

I found a job after about 2 weeks of job hunting. It's with Goodwill Industries. I also have signed up with an office Temporary Service. They haven't placed me yet. So if I can hang with Goodwill, I'll have the Temporary Service take me off of its active file, because I don't like moving from place to place. Right now it's Sunday and I am at one of the malls; just finished my ½-hour walk. George dropped me off at 9:30 a.m. on his way to church. My hours are from 11:00 a.m. to 3:30 p.m. on Sundays (9:30 - 6:00 weekdays). It worked out good this week, because the church has a fellowship dinner every Sunday. (I don't have to cook ---- Goody!)

Since this is the Birth Month of our dear departed Mother, I want to share a few things about Mother that I will always remember. (Charlotte, that tape was truly a blessing. Listening to it brought tears to my eyes, and it doesn't seem that she is gone). I have been dreaming of Mom a lot lately, and the other night I dreamed of Daddy. He looked so tall and handsome with a top coat on and all dressed up, and it seemed that all of us were greeting him with hugs. He didn't say a word; he just hugged each one of us. I don't know what it means. Well, anyway, I remember when we were kids and had no money in the house. It was Christmas time and I remember Mother sitting up all night sewing doll dresses for our old dolls. She may have fixed some other toys for us; I can't remember that. But I'll always remember her sacrificing for us.

I also remember when I was around 9 or 10 years old that I talked back to Mom. She was standing at the sink washing dishes. She didn't say a word, but the next thing I knew, I saw stars. She had taken the wet dish cloth and slapped me across the face. That was the First & Last time I smarted off to Mom. When I was grown, Mother was always there to listen to my woes concerning what I was going through with my marriage. She never offered advice or said you ought to do this or that. She just said, "Barbara, where is your Faith?" She said I could only see so far in front of me, but God sees the entire picture and I just need to Trust Him.

Well, I guess that's all for now. I really miss you all, but it's really nice that I can spend some time with Ken and his wife. And I'm close enough to visit Leonard and his wife. You all have a standing invitation to come visit with us.

Love you much,
Barb

*** * ***

MARSHA WETTER'S Corner

Hi Sisters and Brothers!

This wonderful time has rolled around for us to communicate again. I now get excited to write these letters, to let you know how we all are doing, and to find out what's happening in all of your families. I do hope to find that you all are doing fine and in great spirits. I am doing fine and still working and plan to do so for the next two or three years or until the service center closes down, whichever comes first.

Barb, thanks for the Joyce Meyer tapes. I enjoy them very much! Charlotte, I could not believe the tape you sent us. Just listening to it brought tears to my eyes, to hear Mama's soft and sweet voice again. I had to fuss and demand ("Bring my tape back!") after letting the kids take it home to listen to it. It really brought back memories, and I heard some things I did not know. Mama said we were all good babies and gave her minimal problems, but "wow" when we grew up! Even with our ups and downs, we were still nice kids. ----- Those Holland Kids! Looking down on us (I am sure she is) now, she can turn to her Lord and thank Him for what she accomplished ----- that her kids are doing well, and we did not have to clean houses for a living as she said on the tape.

We all have, or have had, decent jobs, and I know that was because of our teaching and upbringing from Mama and Daddy. We did not then, and do not now, have what you call a whole lot of money, but we were, then and now, happy and well-adjusted children. We are ---- Ladies and Gentlemen ---- with high values and that means a lot in this day and age. I have a picture of Mom smiling down on me in my living room. I look up at it and tell her all the time, ----- "Thanks, and I Love you." Now, all I need is a picture of Daddy. Help me someone, if you have one. I love you all!

Marci

SHARKIE'S Corner

Hey Gang!

Jessie and I gave ourselves a BIG treat the first of this month. We went to see Johnny Mathis! Oh but he was ------ GREAT! We sat there almost spellbound, ----"oohing" & "aaahing" all during the performance. It made us think of you, Butchie ---- he sounds just like you! (smile)

There are SO MANY wonderful memories of Mom. I remember her braiding my hair ----- pulling it tight on the top especially, whenever my tonsils flared up. I remember her being at the old sewing machine, making outfits for all of us girls. Can't recall her sewing pants for the boys, but she probably did. No wonder we have such good cooks and seamstresses in our family. (Me, excluded, of course.)

All those were wonderful memories. But one I will always hold dear to my heart was in the Fall of the mid 80's when she and I went to PTL (Heritage USA) on a Bus Tour. We were the only Blacks on the full bus, and they were all very kind and sweet Christian people. And they really took to Mom. The scenery going through the Great Smokey Mountains was breathtaking!! Mom and I were oohing and aahing and praising The Lord! Mom said, "Oh, I'm so thankful I had a chance to see this kind of beauty!" Little did I know the Alzheimer's was just beginning to take hold of her. To make a long story short, she left the hotel one day when she was supposed to be there resting while I went to some morning meeting. (We would come back and get her for the evening meal and the evening meeting.) I had ordered room service for her breakfast and lunch.) But, she was nowhere to be found when we returned. Everyone searched high and low, and ----- I getting more and more frantic every minute. I just knew whoever brought her room service had tricked her and taken her somewhere, raped and killed her. I had just recently read a book about "The Lost Child" (who ended up murdered), so I was a basket case. And especially when I imagined riding all the way home on the bus without her, and Barb, Cecelia and the others jumping all over me for taking our Mother down there and losing her"!!

But ----- Praise God, we finally went back over to the PTL grounds (we were staying at the Holiday Inn on the highway close by.) and found her. PTL had no Grand Hotel at that time. ----- I had insisted all the time, ----- "she wouldn't go over there without me. She wouldn't know HOW to go over there by herself." But there she was, sitting in a rocker in the Welcome Center, looking at the "Praise The Lord" program on TV. She had forgotten that we were coming back for her. She (who up to then, was busily making certain the door was locked, with all the chains on; checking the windows; and I having to reassure her that we were up high enough that no one could come in the windows) had gotten dressed, gone downstairs to the Lobby and sat outside by the door. When the Shuttle Van got ready to go over to the PTL grounds, someone asked her if she was going over there. She said, "Yes, my daughter is over there." So, off she went, forgetting how BIG a place PTL was. I can just imagine how she was probably sitting with someone just chatting about how nice everything is there, and how glad she was to be there. The shuttle takes everyone to the Welcome Center, then they go wherever they want from there. Thank God, she didn't decide to venture off in some direction or other. Not that she would have been harmed in any way there. But since it was such a gigantic area, it would have really taken a long, long time to find her. When we told her how worried everyone was, she just giggled and said, ----- "Oh, I wasn't afraid. ----- I knew I was on Holy ground." With that, everyone laughed and gave her lots of hugs & kisses. ------ That's our Mom!!

Love,
Charlotte

JENNY'S Corner

Hi Gang!

Here it is that time to get started on February newsletter. Well, I'm going to beat all of you this time (famous words, beat) (smile). I guess that's all I talked about as

Those Holland Kids

I was growing up ---- always wanting to beat on something. Oh well, thanks to my Lord and savior Jesus Christ, He has delivered me from my wicked ways.

In the last couple of months, I've been going back in time when we were all small children and growing up. You know we really didn't have such a bad life. ---- We didn't have everything that we wanted, ---- but I think that Dad and Mom did a pretty good job in rearing us up. There were some bad memories, but through it all, I think the good times made up for the bad times.

Remembering Daddy, I always thought we had the most handsome Dad in the world. I remember watching him shave and brush his hair, and the muscles would just stand out in his arms and I'd think nobody's got a finer daddy than we do. But the Lord chose to take him at an early age. And that left dear Mom to raise up those nine brats by her self. I think she's done a super job! I'm very proud of our family. It took me a long time to accept the Lord and change my life, but I'm so glad I did.

Remembering Mom as her birthday approaches, She was our lifeline as we grew up. She made a vow to God and herself that she would raise her children by herself, with God's help. And she did it. So we should look at ourselves and be proud of who we are and what we stand for, and draw closer to one another, reach out more often, and say we love you. ---- It only takes a few minutes. Let's recapture the close-knit family ties that our dear Mother instilled in us and carry out her wishes that we stand together and be strong. For if we are divided, we fall. I love you all very much and you mean so much to me ----- you'll never know just how much. If we continue following Jesus Christ and not be ashamed of the Gospel of His name, one day we will join our dear parents in that special home that our Lord has prepared for us. The day that we shall behold Him in all of His Glory!!

Love Forever!
Your sister,
Jenny

*** * ***

TWERP'S Corner

Hi Family,
This is a special, special day! I just got through reading the last newsletter. Now I mean it, it gets better and better each time! This one topped it all! It just

blesses my heart to read what all my family is doing. It does make us feel closer.

Family... Charlotte's opening Word was so good and true. Please don't let this become a burden. It's such a blessing. We definitely don't want Charlotte to get discouraged. Charlotte, we really, really appreciate what you're doing, your labor of love. You don't have to do this, but we know you choose to because you love us, and we love you, Sis.

It was so, so good to read Linda, the Author's, letter. Linda, Thank you! That was so encouraging and uplifting, and so grand and professional. Wow! Reading everyone's letters made me smile. But when I got to Donna's, I laughed so hard I thought the kids were going to come up and call the man with the straight jacket. I laughed till I cried. I enjoyed it thoroughly! Donna, I didn't realize you were such a comedienne. You always seemed so proper and straight-laced. (smile) Your drawings are so hilarious! You are good, girl. My, we are learning each other! With all this talent in the family, we should write a book. Seriously!

After I laughed till my sides hurt. I put in my tape from Charlotte, wondering what it was.

Words cannot express my feelings as I heard Mom's voice. Tears once again flowed. I listened to the whole tape and just closed my eyes and envisioned Mom as she talked and giggled and hesitated with her words. Oh how I miss and love her!

I learned so many things that I did not know. Now I remember hearing about my bump on the head, but I didn't know about the stuttering. Also, I didn't know I was sickly. I thank god for my health now. I guess He took pity on me for my sad start. Just listening to how each one was born and the details of Mom and Dad's courtship was indeed precious. Also, Dad's sickness was sad, but enlightening. I already knew he loved us, but this just confirmed it.

Charlotte, you are so special. As I told you on your answering machine, this was the best Christmas present I have ever received. Thank you a thousand times!!!

If this doesn't prompt Kenny and Leonard to get involved in the newsletter, I don't know what will. I love you all very much. And Donna, don't change!

                Love,
                Always,
                Jessie Mae

***** * *****

Those Holland Kids

BUTCHIE'S Corner
No letter received

*****   *   *****

LUCY LOCKET'S Corner

Hello Girls & Boys,

I hope ALL is well with all of you! This issue's date slipped up on me very quietly. ---- It was here before I knew it. I had a particularly rough time the last month and a half, and was going to skip sending my article in this quarter, but when I received Charlotte's card and realized this issue is in remembrance to Mom, so I decided to give it a go.

Marcia, thanks again for your photograph. Now, all I need is Cecelia's and a house to hang them all in. Right? Cecelia ----- did you hear that? Suppose you can get your photo to me before the Lord gets my house to me? -----Wanna Race?

Linda, it was great reading your news article, and it certainly gives our letter a festive touch; ---- keep up the Good Work.

OK. ---- I remember specifically Mom's famous Sunday dinners. They were so special and she worked so hard and seemed to put so much love into each one. I couldn't have enjoyed a meal, fit for a king in a castle, any more than I enjoyed those Sunday meals. I remember the golden-brown fried chicken, so perfectly seasoned and smothered till tender. ----Those Silver Bar creamed peas (anybody else remember Silver Bar peas?) I still make creamed peas occasionally, except they don't sell Silver Bar here in the South. I also remember the sweet potatoes, which are my birthmark ---- the gravy and cornbread dressing. The gravy would get on my sweet potatoes and I liked the taste of the two together, and I eat sweet potatoes and gravy to this day. Now, Mom's grand finale was her "Big Biscuits" ---- nice and flaky and golden brown. ---- Mom could really cook!! She would be serving our food and fussing at us all at the same time. I can imagine how frustrating it must have been trying to keep nine open mouths fed all the time. Did anyone ever compliment Mom on those wonderful meals?

What about her favorite three-cookie recipes? You know: ---- one was a molasses, and another one was a sugar cookie. I can't remember the third one, (I think it was almond) but they were wonderful! Did anyone ever find Mom's recipes? She baked them on Christmas and gave us all an assortment in a decorative tin box. All my kids remember them because they didn't get any. Ha! Ha! I would eat them all and keep them hid until gone. ---- They are still mad at me about those cookies. Every now and then, they remind me of how good the few crumbs were that they tasted. Anyway, if anyone can remember any of the recipes, please let me know!!

As for Mom's "Big Biscuits," I guess the recipe was passed to her from Grandma, because I remember seeing them on her stove. Now, for some reason, I don't remember eating much of anything at Grandma's, but I did see food sitting around her kitchen. I remember drooling at coffeecake or cinnamon rolls on her counters. Now, somebody tell me truthfully, am I having memory blocks or was our "Granny" a wee bit stingy? (smile) OK, OK, maybe it's my memory.

I look back now to the picture of us sitting around the oil stove in the dining room. The old coal-burning stove had been updated to the new oil-burning stove. It was kept burning full blast on those bitterly cold days. I remember one specific day when it was reported as being one of the coldest days of the year. We all were, again, hovered around the stove, and I saw Mom putting water somewhere in the back of the stove to thin out the heat or something. Now, I don't know how old I was, but I decided to help out a little. So I ran and got a glass of water and poured it right into the oil tank when the stove was going full blast. ---- The fire went out and we froze ----. Now, I don't know if I was super young or super stupid, but I remember how everybody glared at me, like I was a small alien from outer space or something. I also remember Mom's exasperation over having to call a service repairman to come out, but I can't remember if it was on a Sunday and they couldn't come right away or what the end results were.

Well folks, I've got more memories, but I will keep them until next time. This time of year in February, I still miss picking up the phone to call Mom and sending her cards and such; there is sweetness in the air, even now.

I am starting to think about a trip home this spring; when I come I'll be staying awhile (Lord willing). Perhaps I will stay one week in Indianapolis and one week in Ft. Wayne.

>   Until Next Time,
>   Love
>   Donna

P.S. Charlotte, I really appreciate the work you are putting into our newsletter. I'm hoping that we have one or two new participants this time. Thanks for your enthusiasm and efforts.

*** * ***

Those Holland Kids

TWIN LEONARD'S Corner
No letter received.
*** * ***

TWIN LINDA'S Corner

Hello Everyone!

Well, it's that time again already. I've been very busy working and trying to get my typing business started and hopefully if God makes the way, I'll have my publishing company successfully running and making big bucks. But, mainly it will inspire and help millions to go another mile and not give up because things look dark and hopeless.

A MOMENT OF REMINISCING ABOUT MOM

The strongest memory I have about Mom, was one of those times when she showed her love, strength, and wisdom: I remember the time when I was in my early, wild, teen years and I came into the house late after being with my girlfriend, Bertha. I was 14 years old or so and she was 19 or 20. She was the bad influence in my life that taught me many of life's dark sides.

I was riding around in the car with Bertha and some of her male friends from Detroit, Michigan. They were all smoking pot and Bertha talked me into smoking. And even though I didn't inhale the two small puffs I took, I had a terrible experience from it.

When my so-called friends dropped me off early that Saturday morning, I was going to sneak up to my room slowly with what was called a monkey on my back. My back and shoulders felt so heavy, I thought I really was carrying a big one on mine.

By the time I got undressed for bed and was about to jump in, I felt my heart speeding fast and pounding loudly in my head and chest. "Oh No, this is it, I'm dying!" I said. I fought back the darkness that tried to envelope me. I nearly went into shock when I saw my blue veins coming out of my hands and arms. I couldn't think of anything except to get downstairs to Momma's bedroom. Then, I felt that everything would be all right. I slowly stumbled down to her room.

Mom sat up with me all night praying for me. She had me repent and to promise God I would serve him.

Well, Mom prayed me through that horrible nightmare. From this day, I will not even be around anyone who smokes, much less smoke anything myself. I don't even smoke cigarettes. God taught me a lasting lesson.

So, if a certain friend of mine ever reads this newsletter, she will understand why I once ran out of her room when she was smoking something that she said relaxes her. I believe it was pot, but maybe she'll know I wasn't judging her; I just don't like being around any kind of smoke. I pray if any of my children ever smoke or drink they, as well, will have a bad experience that will be a lasting lesson to them also.

Yes, I was a wild child who knows that if it wasn't for my mother's PRAYERS, LOVE, PATIENCE, AND STRENGTH, I might not be here today. I want to give the same thing to others in my writings, books, and magazines.

Love Yah All Always!
Twin Linda

CLOSING WORD

Memories ------ Wow! ------ didn't I say this would be Great? But it sure would have been good to have had some input from the male point of view. Must say, I agree with what Jess said: ----- "If this (the tape) doesn't cause the fellows to want to be involved, I don't know what will." So, Brothers, ------ I give up. ------ Evidently, you are just NOT interested. (I really don't know if you heard the tape, for that matter.) But one last thing I will say and then, no more. Everyone is busy these days. Everyone has problems of one sort or another. But being wrapped up in oneself is not the answer. "Reaching out" is still the best therapy for whatever the case may be. Love you both!

And what a sobering thought… "Did, I ever hug Mom and thank her for all those delicious meal, etc.?" It brought tears to my eyes. You are so right; she took pride in putting meals together for us. With so many, you would think she could have just thrown anything together, just to fill our bellies. But I think all you girls (the fellows didn't have a house full of kids) did likewise with your big families. I hope they (your kids) read this and give you your hugs and thanks NOW!

Finally, ----- when I opened each letter ---- the money came falling out! I

Those Holland Kids

got excited and said, ---- Oh, boy, this is fun! Seriously, Thanks to you all for the money toward the expenses.

So let us remember to PRAY ONE FOR ANOTHER. Pray for all our family to be saved. And pray God's healing for all the family. We are seemingly being attacked by Satan in our bodies at this time.

                        See you ----- Next Time, ---- May 1997!
                        Charlotte

chapter 7

May 1997
The thief comes
To kill, steal and destroy

Barbara sits on her favorite soft-colored floral sofa, her usual spot to read and study the Word of God. She enjoys the open view of the front lawn where the cheerful red, white, and deep maroon peonies swaying in the soft morning breeze may help to lift her spirits.

"It's not often," Barbara sighs, "that even after basking in God's Word my soul is still somewhat troubled. Sickness and disease has not been a common occurrence in our family. Aside from the passing of Mom and Daddy (yes, we still refer to him as, Daddy), we have been unusually blessed.

"Now with Cecelia and Venus both struggling to fight off and defeat this enemy called cancer, we find ourselves in a place spiritually that we have never been. We know what Jesus did for us at Calvary. And we have learned from our dear sis Donna's teachings that we must not abuse our temple in which we live.

"Even though many of us have changed our eating habits, unfortunately, others have not. We know our heavenly Father can and often does do miracles. We also know that we must be obedient to His Word. In 1st Corinthians 6:19 He reminds us that our bodies are the very sanctuary of the Holy Spirit who lives in us. So we must bring honor and glory to Him in our bodies. In 1st Corinthians 3:16-17 He prompts us to discern and understand that we are God's permanent dwelling place. And if anyone corrupts or destroys it God will bring him to the corruption of death and destroy him.

"For many years we thought these particular scriptures only referred to the spirit realm. Now most people realize, as do we, that they have dual meaning. I, for one, can see what is happening around the globe to God's own people who don't care properly for their physical bodies or temples. I learned from Donna's teachings that our nation is number one in deaths due to heart disease and cancer. And it is sad to see that the Body of Christ is not exempt from these statistics. We Christians also have been eating ourselves into chronic states of many illnesses and succumbing to terminal diseases.

"Looking back, my cholesterol, blood pressure, and weight were once off the chart. Now after implementing some changes to my diet and taking nutritional supplementation at age sixty-five I am free of all pharmaceutical medications and my weight is where it should be."

Barbara lays her Bible aside and picks up the day's mail. She pulls out the large envelope and opens it, retrieving the pale yellow-colored stapled pages. Her spirit is still grieved, she begins reading.

ISSUE NO. 5
May 26, 1997

OPENING WORD
by Charlotte

Hi Family!

Well, Spring has finally "sprung"! What beautiful weather we are having! For those of you who are in those states where the weather is always nice, this doesn't mean too much to you. But for us Hoosiers, ----- it's a BIG DEAL!

Can you believe it? ---- This is our fifth newsletter! My, but time is going by much too fast. It really does get a little scary when a report comes over the TV and they say this is the second, third, of fourth anniversary of some situation or another. You think, "It couldn't have been that long ago; it seems like it just happened a few months ago or last year." I think God is trying to tell the human race something: ----- "Hurry and get ready, it won't be long!"

Hoping that everyone is doing fine and God is Blessing you and your families. I can hardly wait to read your letters!

***** * *****

BIBBA'S Corner

Hi All,

    I'm starting this letter at work. It's around 3:45 p.m. and 94 degrees outside, and 105 degrees inside this trailer. For those who don't know, I work for Goodwill as an attendant for one of their sites taking in donations. Working at this place is quite an experience. It's hard to fathom how much people spend on clothes for themselves and their children. The toys that come in here are out of site. (I mean sight.) That turned out to be a pun; did you get it? I work at a donation site.

    Oh well, we all can't be a comedian like Cecelia. I know she is talking about me, saying, "Barbara's a real Do-do Bird." As I was saying about all these clothes: I had to interrupt my letter for a minute, because a lady just brought in seven bags (garbage bag-size) of clothing. I realize that some of these things come from yard sales, but most of these people mention that their kids have outgrown the clothes. I remember when Marcia, Charlotte and I were young, the only thing we got for Christmas was a doll, some fruit and candy. We do get some nice things at Goodwill, and these people go to the trouble to fold them, and sometimes put them on hangers. The others bring in their dirty laundry, it looks like. Some of the clothes are so filthy I have to put them in the trash. These are the ones who always want a receipt.

    It's pretty nice out here in Arizona, but I do miss the greenery back home. All you see in yards is dirt and gravel; but the beautiful mountains, palm trees and fabulous sunsets make up for it. However, I plan on going back to Ft. Wayne for a vacation (don't laugh). Since George is not working, I have to do a lot of cooking. I told George that I would be gone for three months, and he said I'd better come back in two weeks. He shouldn't have said that. I told him I was a liberated woman, and he'd better be nice to me. I think he took me seriously, because he's been extra sweet to me lately. (I wonder why.) Well, anyway, we are doing great; I guess old age is mellowing us.

    Well I guess that's it for now. I hope all of my beautiful sisters had a wonderful Mother's Day. Also I wish our good-looking brothers will break down and contribute to our newsletter.

                                   Love and miss all of you,
                                   Barb

Those Holland Kids

MARSHA WETTER'S Corner

Dear Sisters and Brothers,

I hope this letter finds everyone in good health and their families doing well. My family is doing well so far, except for Debra's daughter Venus. Debra and Venus came up to let Venus celebrate her birthday here since she wanted to spend it with family and friends on March 28. Venus had an operation to have some gallstones removed. When she went back to have her after post-surgery examination, the doctor found a lump in her breast. He wanted a biopsy done, but Venus wanted to wait until after she came to Ft. Wayne and then have it done when she got back.

They came on a Thursday of that week and left on Sunday. Friday of that week, she went to the doctor and it showed it was cancer. They removed the lump and the doctor was sure he removed it all. Venus held up very well until the doctor told her she would have to take radiation treatments and it would make her loose her hair and weight ----- then she, kind of, let go.

But I talked to Debra last week and she said Venus is doing better now. The treatments are just until they are sure she has completely shown there are no more signs of the cancer. So we have to remember her in our prayers. I was sorry to hear about Cecelia's problems, though I did not understand when Barbara called me. I had been meaning to call Cecelia.

I want to keep you all up-dated on Brackenridge Street. I went past the other day and all the old houses are gone, all the way back to Douglas Street. Now they have built two-story houses on the other side of Brackenridge and Douglas. They are houses with driveways on the side of the house, leading to the garage. People are living there already. It really looks different over there. Now, for the older brothers and sisters, they had a Central High School Reunion last week at the War Memorial Coliseum. It was not a dressy occasion; you could wear blue jeans or casual dress. I met a lot of friends I have not seen in years. There were a lot of people and it was a real nice gathering. A lot of people asked about all of you, and I told them where you had moved to. It went over so well, they will have another one again, and if they do, I'll keep you posted.

Well, I have rambled on too long now. Guess I'll close this letter, but not before I tell you all I love you! Hi to all------Barb, Jenny, Jessie, Butchie, Donna, Leonard, Linda and you, Charlotte; you're doing a great job. Barb, thanks for sending Boo a card.

With all my Love,
Marci

******   *   ******

SHARKIE's Corner

Hello Again, Everyone!

So glad and thankful to be writing a letter, once again, to my dear family. Thank God that we are all still here enjoying one another. We hear so many tragic things on TV and the news regarding other families, and we just have to say Thank You, Jesus, for watching over us.

Well, let's see, what have we, Jim and I, been doing, and Ritchie, since last we wrote? One thing for sure, ----- we have been BUSY! Can't really say that I've been doing a lot of things, but I just can't seem to catch up. Maybe it's that I'm just slowing down, you think? Really and truly, I just feel overwhelmed! I don't work that many days and hours, but they still seem to interfere with the other projects and personal things I need to do. I like the little job because I work alone and have no boss breathing down my neck. But think I will have to give it up soon.

Jim is still working his job on a part-time basis, usually two mornings a week. But one of the fellows quit, so now Jim has to put in extra days and time until they find a replacement. He does that from time to time anyhow to cover for vacations, etc. And now that the weather is nice, ------ it's back to the golf course! Whoopee!

In April, Jim and I took a weekend bus tour (the same people that Mom and I went with to PTL) to Louisville, KY. It was the opening celebration for the Derby. It was an Air Show down along the Ohio River, (one of the Best we have ever seen.) You know how much Jim loves planes. He was thrilled, to say the least! But when the fireworks began, I thought, ---"You see one fireworks, you seen them all." Ho-Hum. But, how wrong was I! This one was SPECTACULAR!!! I kid you not. I have never seen anything like it in the world! They had fireworks shooting off from barges in the water, fireworks shooting off from the bridge, and the whole bridge was lit up like a waterfall!! People were yelling and screaming! I was shouting, "PRAISE THE LORD! THANK YOU JESUS! for allowing me to SEE such a beautiful sight!" They have it every year, so come on down and go next time. Jessie already said she wants to go.

Then, we just returned from Florida to see Jim's stepsons. We enjoyed Miami this time because it was nice and cool. They said we must have brought the cool weather with us. However, the last two days it was back to typical Miami weather ---- HOT! But then we went on to South Carolina and the weather there was

GREAT, nice and warm but a cool breeze. Back to that later, but first I want to say we drove over to West Palm Beach, Florida, where Cecelia was at the Cancer Treatment Center. My, what a lovely place that was. There were lots of palm trees and plants and flowers around.

Cecelia said, "Yes, it's beautiful, but I'm ready to go HOME!" She had been there for three weeks. And Oh, but she did look GOOD! And had energy she hadn't had in a long time. The hardest thing to get used to, she said, was eating all their food RAW. But the raw corn on the cob was unusually tender and sweet; I tried it and she was right. During the ceremonies for those leaving, each had to say a few words after receiving their certificate. Cecelia gave a good talk, including praise to her Lord, as well as thanking the nice people there for their help. Then they asked her to sing a song. She sang a beautiful song; I think it was "My God is so Good to Me." My, but Cecelia has a beautiful voice!! You could tell that she was "Miss Popularity" there. Everyone really took to her. Cecelia's friend went there also.

Back to South Carolina ---- I Loved It! Wish we could have stayed. It was only 2 1/2 hrs from Atlanta. The place is called Savannah Lakes Resort. Maybe, some day! We stopped over in Nashville and went to my favorite hotel, The Opryland Hotel. One day I hope I can get all us sisters to go there for a couple of days. You don't know what you're missing!! Come on, let's do it! Happy Belated Birthday, Butchie!! I meant to send you a card, but hurried off and forgot. Hope you had a Beautiful Day! Love to you All!

Charlotte

JENNY'S Corner
(No letter received, due to illness.)

***** * *****

TWERP'S Corner

Hi Family,
Gee, can you believe it? It's our fifth newsletter. God is so good! The time always sneaks up on me. I'm sure going to try to have this letter beat Charlotte home.

I don't know if anyone else does this, but I reread the newsletter before I start writing. First, it's because I get enjoyment all over again and second, it brings me abreast on what to respond to in my letter.

Everyone is doing well on this end. Rhonda has already moved to Atlanta and now she has started law school. Melanie has started college to be an accountant. Joey will graduate next month and plans to go to Joliet Jr. College for football and art this fall. Melanie's two kids are also graduating next month. They also are going to college. I'm proud of them all. Gayla, even though married and working, got back into cheerleading. She got accepted to cheer for a pro football team; I forgot the name. Lori and her husband are talking about moving to California. Boy, I hate to see them go so far. But that's life! Leslie is expecting her third child. It's going to be another boy, which makes two boys and one girl. Sure as shooting, Lori will probably be next. She and Leslie stay neck and neck.

I had a great Mother's Day. Tom and I took off for the weekend and had a ball. We didn't go far ---- only to southern Indiana, where we holed up in a motel and rested, rested, rested! We are planning two more trips: -----one to Gatlinburg in July for one week, and maybe, ---- maybe ---- Arizona! Yea!! I can't wait to get back there. If we go, the first thing I'm going to do is bop Kenny upside his big head! First, because he has not written into the newsletter, and second, he hasn't sent my tapes yet!!!

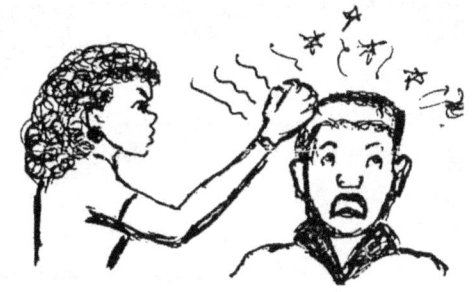

Sisters, and ----- maybe brothers, ----- I plan to do a picture of Daddy and send a copy to everyone. That's a promise. I just have to get motivated. I've been away from my art room ever since I started working and now that the tax season is over, I've gotten lazy! You all help me by staying on me (smile). Finally, Cecelia, it's so good knowing that you're home and on the road to recovery. But not half as glad as Poogie ----- Right Poog?
God bless you, Sis. God is so good.

I'm signing off for now. I love you all so much.
      As Always,
      Jessie Mae

******* * *******

P.S. Here is the notebook cover that Marcie made to hold all of her copies of the family newsletters. It's made of cloth that slips right over a three-ring binder notebook.

The letters are pasted on, and the bows are also made of cloth. It's beautiful, Marcia; please make us one. I'm putting my order in first. Let me know how much. Jessie

BUTCHIE'S Corner
No Letter Received.

******* * *******

LUCY LOCKET'S Corner

Hello, One and All,

I'm trusting that all is well with everyone! The Lord is so good to us all, isn't He? We all are Very Special to Him because Mom, our Dear Mother, was so special to Him, and next to them both, this news newsletter is the best thing that could have happened to us. Mother's spirit is definitely still with us. Praise God for our fifth newsletter!!

This is a very busy time for me. I've got quite a few things going on at once now, and it is difficult keeping up. I keep physical lists on hand or I will usually miss something important. I was reading through earlier newsletters about how our family was so musically inclined.

I miss not having a piano, since I left Ft. Wayne and sold mine. I do believe the Holy Spirit has been urging me to begin singing again; however, all of my background tapes are in storage. When I first came to Atlanta, I sang solos in several churches. Then when Satan beat down my spirit, he also stole my joy and I sang no more. I also remember singing duets and trios with Jessie in McKee Street Church.

Kenny and I sang in school Talent Shows ---- a duet once or twice. So I've decided to buy a couple of accompaniment tapes and begin singing again. Since the Word of God says, "A Merry Heart doeth Good like a Medicine," maybe I'll get completely well!

I made the mistake of not sitting right down after reading our last newsletter, to start on this one, because my thoughts about Mom were flowing strong and I had much more to say. But now, for some strange reason, they are not coming easily, so I won't force them. Maybe the Holy Spirit helps us a lot more during Mom's birthday month. However, I will say that from reading the other issues, I can vividly remember Grandma's back yard. I loved that "peach tree" and that swing. I loved Grandma's entire house; it always was so exciting and mysterious ---- a big adventure with lots of pretty things on tables, dressers, etc. to look at and try to touch when no one was looking.

Cecelia, I know you are happy to be back home, stronger and more nutritionally knowledgeable than when you left. Just remember to get plenty of rest, as rest is the most important ingredient for healing; the body performs its repair work at night and daytime rest periods. Especially though at night when all vital organs don't have food- processing functions going on. I, too, should practice what I preach. ----- Lately, I am terribly rest-broken.

Well Folks, I've got writer's cramps and I'm too exhausted to draw pictures and be witty today. So, farewell, 'till next time.

I Love you All,
Donna

*** * ***

TWIN # 1's Corner
No Letter Received.

TWIN # 2's Corner
No Letter Received.

*** * ***

CLOSING WORD

Wow! What a time I had getting THIS newsletter out. Thought I would never get it completed. What a month! Sounds like everyone is overly busy at this time. What is it? Somewhere in the Bible is something about Satan trying to wear down the Saints of God. And I believe that is exactly what he is trying to do in these last days. Well, let him keep on trying because

Those Holland Kids

that is all he can do, but we won't let him succeed, will we?

In all seriousness, we really have to SLOW down. I know that I intend to do so. I am either going to quit this job completely, or turn some of the stores over to the rep. What happened recently is that I was away on our trip and the other rep was supposed to do my stores, but he quit and nothing got done. So now my boss and I are knocking ourselves out to catch up, as well as training a new rep. So I would come in bone-tired at night and fall into bed. I would then try to get up early (and then couldn't get up as early as I would have liked to) to work on the newsletter.

Barbara called last weekend and said Butchie wanted to send a letter, if it wasn't too late. I agreed to wait on it knowing you all would be overjoyed to be hearing from him, and therefore forgive me for being so late. With the holiday being on Monday and mail probably slow, I waited a little longer into the week hoping the letter would come. But it didn't. I finally had to go on to the closing word and try, now, to squeeze in time to run the letters off and get mailed.

Jessie called and offered her help, but there wasn't anything she could do at that point since it was in limbo so to speak. Now when it came time to run off and assemble, I was too pushed to get it to her, and I know how very overloaded she is anyhow. So, this will not happen again. The newsletter deadline will NOT be overlooked ---- it is not fair to those who get their letter in on time. (Namely Marcia and Jessie. Theirs were here waiting when I returned from vacation.) REMINDER cards will be sent so please post it up.

Barb, hope you don't mind that I sent yours through as you typed it ----- mistakes and all ----- (smile). Well, I had a LOT of errors, also. I couldn't seem to get these fingers to hit the right keys. The only difference is that I used "white-out".

Sounds like your children are doing real well, and Thank God, Ronnie is doing better. Looking forward to seeing you soon, ---- you Liberated Woman!! (smile)
Marcia, we are so sorry to hear about Venus' health problem, but also glad to hear she is doing better. We will add her, specially, to our prayer time.

Thanks so much for keeping us informed on what's happening there in Ft. Wayne, ---- and particularly about our dear Brackenridge Street.

Thanks again for keeping us updated on our "Home Town"!! Oh, how I wish I could have been there for the Central High School Reunion. Yes, please let us know about any future ones. Jessie, yes, your letter beat me home. I mean, that mail sure got a beautiful set of "wings"!! And I hope you all (family) dug that face on the letter! (smile)

You can be sure I'll stay on your case regarding the picture of Daddy. You shouldn't have given us permission. And when you do see Kenny, ----- give him a "bop" for me also! Oh yes, Thanks so much for the beautiful drawing of the Notebook cover!! By all means ----- EVERYONE ---- we do want one of those things, don't we? Marcia, what a talented gal you are!! Let us know ----- HOW MUCH.

Donna, you see how informative this newsletter is? It is revealing all these hidden talents! I didn't know you used to love to sing! I know we all used to open our mouths a lot when we were kids and put on talent shows for Mom and Daddy. But I thought it ended there for us all, except Kenny. Of course, as I mentioned earlier, I just discovered how beautiful Jenny sings. But you and Butchie singing together ----- I never knew that! That would be "wonderful" for you to start again! You are right about not forcing yourself to think of things back when we were young and on Brackenridge Street. When it comes, it will just flow out, especially when we are not so very tired. Yes, I remember Grandma's house, too ---- and, oh yes, it was so much fun to go there. Not only when they lived out in the country on Avondale Drive (those were really the good times), but also when they moved in town on Chute Street. Oh God, how I wish we had video cameras back then!

Linda, don't know what's going on with you. ---- Let us hear from you. Sukie, my long time friend, was saying how inspiring your last letter was. So, you need to write again, ----- OK?

Butchie and Leonard, I'm sending you guys a copy of this newsletter since you are mentioned several times Butch. And hope it will finally whet both your appetites to be a part of this! At least you are a little closer: ----You both now have promised to send a letter…maybe, maybe, maybe ---- next time!

And now, I want to end with words concerning you, Jenny. You know that all of our hearts and love are with you. We want so very much for you to be completely well again. It's like the Word of God says in the Bible regarding the Body of Christ: ---- When one hurts, we all hurt. That is so true. There is not a day that goes by that you are not on our minds, not just during our prayer time, but throughout the day and evenings. Different things that I am doing, I find myself saying, "Oh Lord Jesus, let Cecelia be able to do this again." For those of you who didn't know, we are praying EACH day, not just for Cecelia, but for ALL the family. But we emphasize Cecelia's situation, and now we add Venus, and of course Donna also for complete healing. We added Thelma, Cecelia's friend, since she was there at the Cancer Treatment Center, with Jenny. Isn't this something? How long have we been trying to get a SET time for us to have family prayer? Much TOO Long, I might say. And then it took a tragedy to get us on the ball. Well, at least we are DOING it NOW!

This entire newsletter experience has not been easy for any of us, I know. It has taken a quality commitment, much quality time and effort, as well as a spirit of giving from each of us. And we did it all in the name of our Lord God Jehovah!!

>Bye for now,
>Until next time!
>Love You ALL!
>Charlotte

****** * ******

P.S. again. Since the next newsletter is due out in August, which is close to September, Daddy's birthday month, let's try to remember some more things about him, Daddy and Mother, or just about life on Brackenridge Street. OK?

chapter 8

August 1997
Struggles for health;
the battle begins

"Amazing!" Donna speaks under her breath. "It's been exactly one year and three months since we started our family newsletter." Her thoughts have been at ebb level all morning. Now that she has found her usual spot to relax on the front porch steps she is desperately trying to muster enough energy to walk to the box to check for today's mail. Her small 114-pound frame feels more like 200 pounds of lead.

The crisp morning breeze, usually pleasant this time of year, actually seems a little too chilly. And the quiet calm in the air that should be comforting only manages to usher in an uneasy feeling in the pit of her stomach. The lovely landscape of varying autumn colors and late blossoms bring her no pleasure today.

"Why, oh, why didn't Cecelia stay on the food program that was so effective for her at the Cancer clinic?" The question rolls around in her head. "Jenny knew that if she maintained what she learned there for one year the cancer would go into remission and she would be on the road to complete health. The facts and testimonials that substantiated the success claims of the clinic were the reasons Jenny agreed to go there. Additionally, she became her own testimony. We rolled her in a wheelchair through the airport en route to the clinic. Three weeks later she walked through that same airport under her own power after she sang a parting solo to those she had befriended and was leaving behind.

"Cecelia returned home strong, energized, and in high spirits. I personally believe she felt so well that her flesh deceived her. She thought she could go back to her old ways of cooking and eating dead food and still continue to heal. It didn't take long; the lack of nutrients from being off the raw diet probably caused the dormant cancer cells to become again active. Jenny's strength and energy quickly waned and she took a turn for the worse. That particular clinic has had a track record for many years of curing cancer based on their advice to stay on the raw diet for one full year after leaving.

"The thing that troubles me relentlessly is that Cecelia and I never seemed to have been able to patch up our differences. Even though we love each other that invisible but definite wall between us kept us apart. The enemy wouldn't allow us to forget certain events of the past that impacted our relationship. We both were married at the time, but neither of us had a strong relationship with the Lord so we were equally at fault.

"As I look back at the incidents we allowed Satan to use against us, they clearly were insignificant molehills that we both mistook as impassable and insurmountable mountains."

The sound of an approaching vehicle breaks the sickening silence. When the mail truck comes into view Donna pulls herself up. The driver stops. Donna manages a pseudo-cheery hello and he hands her a large stack of mail.

Donna bypasses her spot on the steps and makes her way into the house. She chooses, instead, the muted berry-colored lounger off the living area. The open view of the rear landscape and the burst of colors are not her main focus this time. The plush comfort of her favorite reading chair is what she needs today.

She tears open the large envelope. The bold, tangerine color of the stapled pages is surprisingly uplifting. Donna settles back a little further into the soft cushions and begins reading.

Those HOLLAND Kids
THEN and NOW

"Bibba" – "Marsha Wetter" – "Sharkie" – "Jenny" – "Twerp" – "Butchie" – "Lucy Locket" – "Twins" – "Barbara" – "Marcia" – "Charlotte" – "Cecelia" – "Jessie" – "Kenneth" – "Donna" – "Leonard" – "Linda"

ISSUE NO. 6
August 26, 1997
(Extended into Sept.)

OPENNG WORD
by Charlotte

Hi Dear Family:

Well, Thank God, we did get our newsletter together. This has been a really trying time for everyone, ---- as individuals as well as a family. So many attacks coming from the enemy of our souls: sickness, financial problems, tiredness, and being overly busy and burdened.

We have mostly been concerned for our dear sister Cecelia (JENNY). Although she is the one who has been feeling the pain and discomfort, personally in her body, we have been going through pain and discomfort in our minds and in our souls. We have been in intense BATTLE, and no battle is fun, or easy. But, we would not think of giving up or jumping ship ---- NO, NO, NEVER! Because first of all, we KNOW WHO is in this battle with us: ---- our CAPTAIN, ---- JESUS -----THE ONE who NEVER FAILS ----- CANNOT FAIL!! And, If we all would TRUST Him and His WORD more, we wouldn't experience all the agony and frustration we put ourselves through. I don't know as yet what each one is saying in her letter, but I hope it (this newsletter) will prove to be a healing balm for us all, ---- and ESPECIALLY for you, Cecelia!

BIBBA'S Corner

Hi Everybody,

I started to bypass writing for this newsletter because of all that has happened since the last letter. It seems as though the devil was using his trump card on some of the family, but Thank God, that was the best he could do. Praise God our Lord and Savior came through!

Donna and I talked about not feeling up to writing this month. Then, the Holy Spirit came into our conversation and convicted both of us. We have beautiful testimonies of God's Grace, Mercy and Faithfulness that need to be shared with the rest of the family.

Before I go into what the Lord did for Ron, and also for me, I want to pay tribute to our Dad whose Birthday is Sept. first, with a couple of incidents when we were kids. On the serious side, Mom and Daddy took me, Marcia, Charlotte and Jenny (who was a baby at the time) to a lake in Rome City, Indiana. We spent the night there so that Mom and Dad could fish. The next morning we had a breakfast of bologna sandwiches and cold pork & beans. Boy, was that ever

Those Holland Kids

good! Then Daddy took Marcia and I for a boat ride. While out in the middle of the lake, a storm came up. Daddy was trying to row the boat back to shore, but was having a difficult time with the wind, rain and rough water. From what Dad told us later, he was really scared but did not let us know it at the time because we kept looking at him. He acted as if everything was going to be OK and that we would make it back to shore. When we saw that Daddy wasn't worried, we were confident and not afraid. I know now that God was with us and took care of us. Our dad was a very wise man even though he wasn't saved at the time. (At another time I will share with you about how Dad got saved.)

On another occasion, one of us did something we shouldn't have, but we wouldn't tattle on one another. Since no one would own up to it, Dad lined us all up in the kitchen and whipped every one of us. When I was about 12 or 13 years old, I thought I was in love and wrote a letter to a boy named Lenny, and put it in a cabinet till I could give it to him. Daddy found it. He lectured me first and then beat the stew out of me. It's funny now, but it wasn't then. We had wonderful parents and I'm so glad they are with the Lord and enjoying the ultimate life!

Now let me share with you something about Ron's ordeal. On July 19th I was helping Ron move into his new apartment, when he began complaining of a bad headache. He took some Tylenol and said he was going to try to go to work on Saturday. I didn't hear from him at all and I couldn't get to his apartment because of the locked security door on the outside of the complex. I had a premonition on Sunday that something was terribly wrong, so I prayed for Ron and asked the Lord to take care of what might be wrong. On Monday afternoon I went to his apartment and it took a long time for him to open the door, and he looked terrible. He said he had a bad headache and was dizzy.

I then took him over to Medical Emergency Room. After he lay there for about four hours, they finally took him to X-ray. Then it took them almost two hours to read the X-rays. (They had taken a CAT scan) There was only one doctor on duty and it was really busy. The diagnosis was a severe sinus infection and the doctor prescribed antibiotics, pain pills and decongestant. Ron took the medicine for three days, but he wasn't getting any better. So I decided to call his family doctor. The doctor said Ron needed to get an MRI and a spinal tap. It looked like it might be meningitis, the doctor said. He referred Ron to a neurologist the next day. The neurologist had him admitted to the hospital that same day. This was on Friday, the 25th of July. Just before I got him inside to see the neurologist, Ron was so weak he could hardly walk and asked me if I could go find a wheelchair. While I was inside the building trying to find a wheelchair, Ron was sitting on a bench in front of the building. When I came back, Ron said,

"Mom, I can hear you, but I can't see you." I then called out to the Lord and also rebuked that blindness, in Jesus' Name. I told him to hold still and I would try to find someone to help get him inside. The nurse came out and helped me. When we got inside, his sight came back. By the way, I got ahead of myself. This all happened before the doctor said he needed to be admitted into the hospital.

They finally got Ron a room. It was around 7p.m. when he got settled in. I also know that Ron hadn't been to the bathroom all day. I asked the nurse to use a catheter on him because he wasn't able to go to the bathroom on his own or use a urinal. So, around 11:00 p.m. I asked the nurse again. They felt his stomach and said his bladder wasn't full. They still ignored my plea about a catheter. They took him to get an MRI around 11:30 p.m., brought him back and said he wouldn't lie still. Their plans were to get a spinal tap done right after the MRI. So now, Ron was back in his room. (Earlier he had some V-8 juice and ice cream after he was in the hospital, because he hadn't eaten all day.)

I decided to spend the night with him. Ron fell into a deep sleep. The nurses tried to wake him and checked his pupils ---- they didn't dilate at all. Then the nurse decided to put a catheter in him and called for the doctor. It took about 10-15 minutes before the doctor arrived. While the doctor was on his way, I went over to Ron and called to wake him up, but no response. Then I saw what looked like blood coming from his mouth. I then yelled for the nurse. They wouldn't let me back in the room. Another nurse took me to the next nurses' station, and all the time I kept repeating over and over, "Ron will live and not die." I said, "I don't care what it looks like, I'm not accepting it."

Every scripture that I knew came up before me and I claimed God's Promises. About five minutes later the nurse came and said it wasn't blood, but he had vomited up the V-8 juice. I praised the Lord for answering prayer. Finally, Dr. Shah (he's a Hindu doctor and very nice) came and told me that he had a CAT scan taken and found that Ron had blood clots in the brain. He said, "I'm so glad I didn't give him a spinal tap because that would have killed him instantly." I, also, had prayed previously that God would give the doctors wisdom. Praise God, He did!

They had to operate right away, at 2 a.m. Saturday morning. The surgeon said he couldn't promise anything, but said suctioning the clots out was less dangerous than removing them surgically. Those two hours during surgery felt like an eternity. The Holy Spirit was truly comforting me and telling me to speak ---- Life ---- to Ron, because life and death are in the tongue. (Prov. 18:21) Finally, around 4 a.m. the surgeon came in and wouldn't look at me and sat down on the couch and said the surgery went well. In fact, when they made the incision to put the tubes in, ---- the clots had already liquefied, and just spewed out. Actually, God performed the operation! "Hallelujah!!

The doctors and nurses were so amazed that Ron's countenance has so improved in just a few minutes. They said they never saw anything like it. He was in intensive care for two days. During those two days, he was talking and holding conversation with me, the nurses, and visitors. The only thing was that he lost his sight and short-term memory. He only remembers things prior to his getting sick. He was released from the hospital on Aug. 6th and is doing fine. The doctor said his blindness would be permanent because he suffered a stroke to his optic nerve. But we wouldn't accept permanent blindness and stood against it in Jesus' Name. Now, a month later, his sight is coming back gradually. He can see things up close and he can see things in the sunlight (but not clearly). I give all praise to The Lord Jesus!

Through all of this, The Lord has kept me in perfect peace. Yes, I was concerned, but I continued to trust the Lord and His Promises. He kept my blood pressure normal ----- and that had to be the Lord. Let's continue to pray one for another and God's Will for us to prosper and be in health as our soul prospers. (III John, verse 3)

Barb

*** * ***

MARSHA WETTER'S Corner

Hi Everyone!

Once again, the time has rolled around for the newsletter. Funny as it may sound, I really do not have any news to write about. Everyone in my family is doing fine.

Debra said Venus is doing better and I guess she is adapting to her condition a lot better. I am still working. I have to work every Saturday, which cuts down on my weekends, and I have not enjoyed my summer much. I have two weeks vacation coming up, the last week in August and the first week in September. Maybe I'll get to do some of the things I'd like to do before the summer is over. I know you all are going to wish me a Happy Birthday on August 22nd, and so I am thanking you in advance (smile). My, are we growing old! I'm not going to tell you all how old I'll be, but if you count down, you'll figure it out. I can't believe it, ---- but I am!

I was sorry to hear about Ron and Cecelia. We have enough faith in the

Lord, as a family, that I know He will touch them and pull them through their sickness. I hope we hear from Linda, Leonard and Kenny this time, to see how they are getting along.

I hope everything is going fine in the rest of your families, and the Lord is bestowing plenty of Blessings. We just have to keep praying for Ron and Cecelia that they will recover soon. I am going to close this letter by letting you all know I love you very much, and give honor and remembrance to Mamma and Daddy.

Love you all,
Marci

SHARKIE'S Corner

Hey Everyone!

Beautiful, beautiful Fall is here!! Oh, how I love the cool, crisp autumn days and nights. And before too long, the leaves will be turning their beautiful colors. God really knows how to do things Well! I am learning how to pray at all times and Praise the Lord for everything. I walk or drive here and there and just tell Jesus how wonderful this is and how great that is, and Thank Him for them. Then I always add ---- "Thank you Jesus for granting Cecelia another opportunity to enjoy this again. Thank you that she will again go for walks feeling the sun and the cool breeze, and give Thanks to You with each step she takes. That she can jump in her car again and run to the grocery and do her own shopping again. That she will piddle around her house doing her housework again, cook her meals again!! Praise The Lord, Thank you Jesus!! I kid you not, going through this battle with her has (or is) teaching me to stop murmuring and complaining. If we take stock of how many times we are tempted to murmur and complain about the most trivial things. Really, it is pathetic.

Let me see, what can I remember about Daddy to share with you? Can't think of any one specific incident, that I have not already shared in a previous newsletter issue. I just remember what a handsome man he was. What a talented man he was. He could do just about anything (just like Butchie). Remember when he put the sidewalk in on Brackenridge. We kids were all standing around looking at him work. If I'm not mistaken, he wrote his initials and the year in the wet concrete. I remember him playing the piano and other instruments and writing music for them. I remember him loving to read and having Mom read to him. I remember him loving basketball games and having Mom listen for him if he was not home to hear it on the radio, and she had to keep score for him. I

Those Holland Kids

remember him talking on the phone to some businessperson and talking so intelligently. I remember him caring about us and taking time to sit and listen to us perform our talent. I remember how much he loved potatoes ----- (spuds, as he called them. So Mom would fix them every way possible: ----- Fried (his favorite way), mashed, scalloped, boiled, and baked. I remember how he loved oysters and would eat them raw, and right out of a big can. I just have so many wonderful memories of Daddy ---- yes, even the whippings, which I'm sure I needed.

I remember, also, when Daddy died I couldn't cry until a few days later ----- then it all came out! Guess I was in some sort of shock. I remember Grandmother Susie Wright, (she remarried) Aunt Sarah and Aunt Jessie coming from Detroit. I was thinking that they were still very beautiful, even as they were years ago; they had come to our house when we were kids ---- the time that Daddy was in the hospital. Even though I was very small, I will always remember their smiles, as they played with me ----- one held my hands, the other held my ankles and they would swing me back and forth, as they sang a little song. Grandmother Susie was such an elegant, regal-looking woman. Barb and I did get a chance to meet her, a couple of times, when we went to Detroit, after we had become adults ---- she was still beautiful and queenly-looking. We never, however, met our Grandfather, Berl Holland.

Well, what else have we done since May? In July we went to one of my favorite places-----Mackinac, Island, Michigan. I could positively stay there forever, while on this earth, that is. That is if I could afford to have a home up on the hills overlooking the beautiful blue waters. On that island, no automobiles are allowed, the transportation is only---- walking, bike riding, and sitting in horse-drawn carriages. It is so neat not to be bothered with cars, trucks, etc. Then in August we went to Branson, Missouri, again. They keep sending us those free accommodation offers which we can't seem to resist. All we have to do is go through a couple hours of sales tours on their condos. They are absolutely gorgeous, so that is not too hard to deal with.

In June, I went and spent a week with Cecelia to help her get some much-needed rest. Just before I was to come home, she was stricken with pain in her leg. It was so excruciating that she could hardly move at all on her own. The night before I was to leave, I called out to the Lord: ---- "Please do something! She can't lie here on her bed and not be able to get to the bathroom and do some things for herself!" Praise God, the next morning she was able to get out of bed on her own and get around some. But also, Praise God, that was when Barbara returned from Arizona. And since she lives around the corner, she has been that

Angel of Mercy coming to Cecelia's aid. I really Thank The Lord for our "Big Sis." I don't know what we would do if she were not there close by Cecelia.

Until Next Time!
Love Charlotte
****** * ******

JENNY'S Corner

Hi Everyone,

I'm sending this letter by way of Jessie. I'm not strong enough yet to write, but by the Grace of God, in a couple of weeks, I will be able to write myself.

First of all, I want to thank all of you for your prayers and support. It means so much to me. Most of all, I Thank The Lord for carrying me through. Without Him, Barb, and Poogie, I don't know what I'd have done.

As of today, I am on my way to total recovery. I still have a lot of pain, but the Lord is with me through it all. I have a wonderful, pretty, young nurse ---- my daughter, Tonya. She surprised us all with her nursing skills. She gives me my medication and baths, and sees to my every need. I'm truly blessed. James has also been a great help, as well as my foster daughter, Ellen.

Yesterday I was able to feed myself. This really excited Tonya; she's telling everybody! She also motivates me to keep trying. When I do something stupid, she talks about me, laughs at me and makes me laugh at myself and push harder. Sounds like me, don't it?

So long for now,
Love,
Cecelia

****** * ******

TWERP'S Corner

Hi Gang,

My, my! It's hard to believe that summer's about over and we're into Fall already! A lot has happened in these few months since our last newsletter.

As usual, I reread the newsletter and smiled and chuckled all over again as I refreshed my memory from the reading. It seems everyone was very busy at that time. Charlotte's closing remarks were for us to slow down, especially herself......!

Those Holland Kids

Well Charlotte, did you cut back on any stores? Sisters, and... (brothers?), have you slowed down any? Whoopee...Hallelujah, I have! Do you know what I learned? Those two letters ----N & O work wonders. I'm finding out that I don't have to say "yes" to everyone's request. A question gives the option of answering yes or no. And I'm actually fixing my mouth and hearing the word "no" come out and ------ not allowing guilt to beat me up afterwards.

All the little and big birds have left our --- Nest --- to build their own nests, and Mama and Papa bird are "ecstatic"! Charlotte and Jim have to look around when they come over to make sure they have the right house. We wanted our birds to build their own nests, but Lori and family took it a bit too far. They did move to Santa Ana, California. They left here Tuesday, August 26th, in a 24-ft U-Haul truck. As of this morning, Saturday the 30th, they are about five hours away from their destination. Praise God! Those two young ones learned how real God is, because He showed them many blessings, mercies, and miracles on their journey.

Boy, I'd better slow down a little here. I didn't realize I wrote so much. Before I forget, Marcie, please make a cover for my Family Newsletter Album. Use any color and let me know how much. I'm putting my order in first. Be sure to include the price of postage.

Let me squeeze in my memories of Brackenridge Street. What I remember best about Daddy was we kids and Dad sitting on the front steps at night. We little ones were stretched out, looking up at all the stars. Daddy was telling us how those days were the best days of our lives and we should enjoy them. I remember thinking, "What is he talking about? Me, with all my young problems, how could this be?" All I wanted to do was grow up fast. Oh Daddy, how right you were! You'd better believe I said the same thing to my children.

I also remember when Daddy bought Butchie a whole loaf of bread. (Kenny loved plain bread.) Kenny ate the whole loaf and did not share one piece with anyone ------- Greedy! I also remember when Donna and I were throwing our homemade ball, (clothes wrapped in a wad and tied with a belt) in the house. ----- Mom had warned us over and over about that. Well, my goodness, we just wanted to have a little fun. We were going to be careful not to break anything, and besides, Mom was nowhere around; she would never know. Smart thinking, right? ---- Wrong! I tossed it to Donna. Donna missed. ---- CRASH, BANG, there went Mom's lamp! You talking about some bony legs trembling. ----- Yep, Mom got me! She held me by one bony arm and started switching my skinny legs. Thank God we wore dresses in those days. I remember so well after a couple of licks, my little legs folded up under my skirt like wheels under a plane and my skirt sheltered most of the licks. I think my ego got hurt the most. I remember lying down on the couch rocking my head from side to side, crying and saying (very softly): ---- "I hate Mama, I hate Mama!" After a few tears I was up and around and loving Mom again! Oh youth!!!

Well, I'm really closing now before Charlotte strangles me! Family, I love you all so much that it hurts. I thank God for all of you. Especially, Cecelia!

So Long for now,
Jessie Mae

*** ** ***

BUTCHIE'S Corner

Heard that he had a letter written last time and didn't send it because he thought it was too late. He was supposed to send it this time. What happened Ken?

*** ** ***

LUCY LOCKET'S Corner

Hi Everyone!!

It's time again to share in each other's lives ---- time to open up our hearts if need be. These times are not always joyful for us, but we can cry with each other and laugh with each other. My prayers are with you, Cecelia, as we are trusting in The Lord for your healing and wholeness; for we know that He alone is able and requires no help.

As for the rest of us (and mostly, I'm speaking for myself), we must not allow our personal trials and schedules to stop the progress of what The Lord has started through our (His) newsletter. I believe that as Satan tries to come against our family, The Lord will use this "Holland Newsletter" to serve as a "Bonding Glue" of sorts, as a source of comfort and fellowship for us in times of tribulation.

So please, "Girls and Boys," don't allow Satan to discourage us from picking up that pen or taking the cover off of that typewriter or computer during those times. Even as trouble is always at the door, The Lord God our Faithful Savior, is still on the throne and is still in the miracle-working business. One of my favorite scriptures is Psalm 27:

The Lord is (our) light and my (our) salvation;
  Whom shall I (we) fear?
The Lord is the stronghold of my (our) life;
  of whom shall we be afraid?
Though a host encamp against me (us),
  yet I (we) will be confident.
One thing I (we) have asked of The Lord,
  and that I (we) seek after;
That I (we) may dwell in the House of The Lord,
  all the days of my (our) life (lives);
To behold the beauty of The Lord,
  and to inquire in His Temple.
For He will hide me (us) in His Shelter in the day of trouble;
  He will conceal me (us) under the cover of His tent.
He will set me (us) high upon a rock,
  and now my (our) head is lifted up above my (our) enemies
    round about me (us).
And I (we) will offer in His tent
  sacrifices with shouts of joy;
And I (we) will sing Praises and make melody to The Lord.

Barbara and I were talking one day and were complaining about the lack of time available to prepare our articles, when I realized that we had just finished sharing with each other about a miracle The Lord had worked in both of our lives. I told Barbara we both ought to be ashamed because we have something wonderful to share with the family. So, here is my testimony!!

I had been believing The Lord for a $2,400 Miracle, which I needed before the 20th of August. Barbara was on a spiritual high, from the miracle the Lord worked in her life, so she suggested that we agree in prayer and claim the $2400 for me. I said "OK" even though I had by that time pretty much given up, because all of my sources had seemingly dried up.

So Barbara, being really fired up, called out to The Lord, and by the time she finished, I was a believer again. Now, I had been trying to sell my computer and color printer to come up with part of the money, even though I really preferred to keep it. And wouldn't you know The Lord worked it out so that the $2,400 situation was resolved for $1,800, which He provided, and I was able to keep my computer. Praise The Lord!! Isn't He Wonderful?

I know this newsletter was supposed to be partly dedicated to Daddy, but I don't remember anything about Daddy; I only know what I've heard you all speak about.

You all may as well know that this newsletter is quite a Miracle in itself. I just couldn't see how to fit it into any day. I've had quite a summer: training for the new business, watching and tutoring three grandchildren and occasionally four grandchildren five days a week. Also, I moved out of Teresa's house, as planned, and am maintaining my existing business. Oh yes, and I was also making business calls and setting appointments for my "X", Mel ------ Yes! He paid me. (smile) But I'm doing ----------"ferfectly pine" --------I mean, "perfectly fine"---------- really (smile)

Bye Yah All!!
Donna

TWIN #1's Corner

Although Leonard did not submit a letter, he had some very profound words, when I talked with him by phone. He said he had a feeling that something was not just right at home. He said the main thing Cecelia and all of us must be on guard against is---- FEAR!

He said the devil will use Fear against us and thereby keep our Faith from being strong. He said a lot more and I wanted him to write it all down for the newsletter, but he wasn't sure he would be able to do so. Wish I'd had my tape recorder handy at the time. Oh well, anyhow, it was good WORD and worthy to take heed to. Thanks Brother! We Love You.!

*** ** ***

Twin Linda's Corner

HI EVERYONE, LOVE YOU!

Well, everything is calming down and it seems that maybe I'll survive. (smile) Marcus has two jobs and plans to get his GED. We're busy selling HERBAL products, which has changed my life! I have lost 11 pounds since I started taking and selling the products, August 8th.

Stephanie is recovering well from her operation on her foot and is in good spirits. I just pray that she will get over her bitterness so she will fall in love with God.

Neva is going to have a boy in December and we're all excited. I'm happy to have my baby girl back home. God has really turned things around for us. We are really close now. I thank God every day for her and Stephanie. I thank God for my handsome boys too.

My prayers are with Cecelia, Ron and Venus. I love you, Cecelia. Hurry and get well, Sis. I know God is going to do a marvelous, wondrous, work in and for you! You're going to be happier than you have ever been in your whole life! God has a miracle for you. Claim it, believe it, and don't give up. Don't be stubborn when God shows you something wrong in your thinking and living. Be willing to let it go and set yourself free.

I can't tell you anything about Daddy because I never saw him except in photos. I can only remember dreaming about him. I often wondered why he left before Leonard and I got to know or see him.

That's about it. Everybody take care, and Charlotte, thanks for the order and I'll be getting that out to you soon. I'm still learning the ropes. Barb, thanks for your help toward my rent. I appreciate it.

*** ** ***

CLOSING WORD

Well, Praise God!! Weren't these letters WONDERFUL?? And could we not see and feel the Love of The Lord in each of them? I tell you, I could hardly contain myself at the typewriter! The Faith in the words of each of you was astounding! How can Satan possibly THINK he will win over each and every one of these circumstances? NO WAY ------ THE LORD IS ON OUR SIDE! Praise The Lord!!

Barbara, thanks for the contribution to the newsletter expense, but I will return your check. You have extra expenses since taking care of Ron, and even buying some things for Cecelia. Thanks for sharing that wonderful miracle and tell Ron to keep Praising God! And I remember that boat incident: ----- Mom was on the shore yelling for Daddy to come back!

Marcia, put me down, also, for a Newsletter Cover. I'm printing it again on the back of this newsletter just to remind everyone about it.

Cecelia, I had typed a little message in your spot saying why you did not submit a letter. Then when I opened Jessie's envelope and saw your letter, ---- I was overjoyed! I'm sure everyone is happy to see yours also. I know you feel the love and prayers and faith going out and up to the throne on your behalf. Continue to believe and claim and Thank God for your healing, ----- and the manifestation WILL come in God's timing!

Jessie, thanks for being the messenger for Jenny's article. It was a pleasant surprise! You're right: It is hard to get used to that ---- LOUD SILENCE ---- when we come to your house. I usually prepare myself for "Grand Central Station," ---- and then I get the shock treatment!! (smile) I'll just have to send "Little Ricky" over every now and then to "shake" things up for you and Hubby ---- just so you won't get too lonely!! Girl, you really "cracked me up" about that whipping!! You didn't have to fret yourself about your letter being too long. You forgot that Donna's was coming along, ---- and there was NO WAY any of you can compete with her manual with all those "cute" little drawings! (smile)

Donna, you are a "trip"!! I tell you, I always take my "break" just before digging into your letter. ---- I know I'm in for it! I'm sure that 27th Psalm blessed everyone as it did me. Thanks for reminding us of it. Thank The Lord, also, for your Miracle, --- and thanks for sharing it with us! Looking forward to your visit here next weekend!!

Linda, after Donna's letter ---- I was 'sure nuf' tired. So, seeing your beautifully typed letter was Joy! Joy! (just kidding, Donna) Thanks for getting one in this time. Good to hear about the children. And we will all be pulling for you and praying that your business is successful! We will be, especially, praying for Stephanie, that she will come to know Jesus in a very wonderful and special way!!

In closing, ---- let us all do what we heard and read in this issue of our newsletter. Let's make certain that our thinking and living is RIGHT before God ---- asking Him to reveal to us anything and everything. Let's put

Those Holland Kids

FEAR away from us, realizing that God is on our side! Let's keep Praising The Lord! Standing on His Word! Claiming His Promises! And most of all: ---- GET MAD AT THE DEVIL and say as Barbara did, ---- "NO, NO, you won't take our sister, Cecelia," and all the other things we are praying for.!! Let's stand in AGREEMENT about all these things. Lets bombard Heaven for Cecelia, Poogie, Tonya and the other children in that family ---- and WATCH God perform surgery on Cecelia!!!

Charlotte

chapter 9

November 1997
Losing the battle but winning the War

Seated at the window, Jessie has a clear view of the mailbox. She has been there for a while anxiously awaiting the truck to arrive with the current issue of the newsletter. "I'm really concerned as to how the family is holding up," she says, speaking barely above a whisper. She hears the motor and before the truck rolls up she is on her feet and out of the door. Within seconds, she bolts into the house carrying a bundle of mail with a large envelope conspicuously visible.

Jessie settles for the first chair in her pathway, collapses into it, and lifts the sea-green-colored stapled pages from their protector and begins reading.

ISSUE NO. 7
NOVEMBER 26, 1997

OPENING WORD
by Charlotte

Hi Again Family:

Well, Sisters & Brothers ----- hope you all are coming along OK, dealing with the loss that has occurred in our family. Our dear Sis, Cecelia, and Marcia's Granddaughter, Venus. I was hoping everyone would send in a letter this time to have some thoughts regarding the loss of our loved ones. I haven't read any of the letters yet, as I write these opening words, but do know how many letters are a part of this newsletter.

I kept thinking that the newsletter wouldn't be the same without Cecelia. It really doesn't seem the same. But thanks to Marcia again, for being

Those Holland Kids

"Right on Target." Her letter is always here right on the date requested. Barb's was in the next day. Jessie got the date mixed up, because I told her by word of mouth and didn't send a reminder card. I told Linda when I talked with her, but didn't send a reminder card. Donna was supposed to call and remind her. Donna called on the due date and expressed regret that she just couldn't get herself together to do a letter this time. She said that she is "too long-winded" to just send a short letter, as I suggested. But, come on, Donna, everyone would rather hear a few words from you than no words!

That also goes for the other "missing links." I was pleasantly SURPRISED with calls (she had to call several times before catching me at home) from Judy. She expressed how very much she and Butchie enjoy the newsletter, and said to please not take them off the mailing list. They are hoping that they will be able to participate in the next newsletter after the first of the year, ---- which will be February. She said they just have been overwhelmed, but things should get back to normal by then. Got a chance, at that time, to speak with brother Butch ---- my, he sounded Good! Come on, Leonard and Wilma! Please, don't miss the next newsletter; ------ let me hear from you guys! Leonard did call each of us, after Cecelia's passing, and it was REALLY sweet talking to him. I do miss you fellows and wives and kids so very much. Hope Jim and I can make a visit out that way soon.

So, sit back and enjoy our smallest newsletter to date.

BIBBA'S Corner

Greetings to All of You,

Well, right now in Ft. Wayne, we are experiencing a winter wonderland. Our first snow of the season appeared on Friday, Nov. 14th. I am homesick for the beautiful weather and mountain scenery of Arizona. Most of all, I miss the fellowship with you, Ken and Judy. Hopefully, we'll see you this time next year!

After all the trials over the last few months, God in all His Mercy has given me a Peace and Rest that is hard to describe. It says in Psalms 107: 24 – 31,,,,,,,,

They saw the works of the Lord,
His wonderful deeds in the deep.
For He spoke and stirred up a tempest

> that lifted high the waves.
> They mounted up to the heavens
> > and went down to the depths;
> > in their peril their courage melted away.
> They reeled and staggered like drunken men;
> > they were at their wits end.
> Then they cried out to the Lord in their trouble,
> > and He brought them out of their distress.
> He stilled the storm to a whisper;
> > the waves of the sea were hushed.
> They were glad when it grew calm,
> > and He guided them to their desired haven.
> Let them give thanks to the Lord for His unfailing love
> > and His wonderful deeds for men.

God has also Blessed me in that He allowed Marvin to make a trip out here in October. He flew into Indianapolis on Oct. 21st, and spent the night. We (Ron, Marvin and myself) drove to Pittsburg for a reunion with Crystal and Anthony. That was the first time we were all together since everyone went their separate ways. It was a beautiful family reunion. Ron is doing fine and is improving every day.

> *Thanks so much for your prayers.*
> *Barb*

****** * ******

MARSHA WETTER'S Corner

Hi Sisters—and Brothers:

(I want to know if these letters are also being sent to the brothers!)

This is the hardest letter of all to write. Appropriately so, since it should be in remembrance of our Beloved Sister Cecelia, who is no longer with us— only in our saddened hearts. Even as I write this letter, it brings tears in my eyes, knowing there will not be a letter from her to read. The only thing that consoles me is that I am sure she is in a better place. She, Mama and Daddy and the rest of our loved ones are looking down on us, trying to make it through this struggle-

stricken world.

My Special Letter to Cecelia:

I will always remember the good times we had together. I am sorry we were not closer, as we grew older, but understanding we each had our own life to live. Even so, Cecelia, you were deeply loved and I will miss your unusually witty and wise contributions in my life.

I have to keep going. I will start on my project to get the notebooks out to you all (now, minus one).

Due to the weather, my hours at work are cut down and I promise to get them to you before the end of the year. Maybe it will be my Christmas present to you all.

Leonard called and talked to me, and it was good hearing his voice after so long, and he and his family are doing fine. It was nice seeing you, Donna, when you were here in Ft. Wayne. Kenny, I hope you and your family are doing fine. Tell Judy and the girls and their kids I said "Hello."

I am sorry this was such a sad letter. I hope the next one will be better. I am wishing all of you a very nice Thanksgiving, a Merry Christmas, and a very Happy New Year! Until the next letter,

I love you all.
Marci

****** * *******

SHARKIE'S Corner

My Dear Sisters & Brothers,

How much I appreciate you ----- more than ever before. Cecelia's sickness and passing really hit me hard. It was so difficult seeing her suffer. We had such great hope when she went to the Natural Healing Cancer Institute in Florida last April. She looked great and felt so much better when leaving there. But then things started going downhill. Little did we all realize that in six months she would be gone from us. Two weeks prior to her leaving us, Donna drove up from Atlanta, and we all went to spend a week with Jenny. (Thank The Lord for that time with her.) We were there to be with her and help her, ---- not thinking of her dying.

Being around her we didn't, at least I didn't, notice completely, how close to death she looked. But, Melanie (Jessie's daughter) took a snapshot of her at that time. Jessie and I didn't see it until later, and ---- we were shocked at how very thin she was, with sunken eyes. But for those of you who were not at the funeral, ---- she was absolutely BEAUTIFUL!! She looked as though she never had a sick day in her life. The Beauty & Peace of The Lord was definitely on her. She just looked asleep.

But since her leaving us, I have been missing her so very much. I miss her calling me and me calling her. I miss her comical remarks about things and how she could make me laugh. Until recently, each time I would see certain types of people --- like real old people, or people who look like thugs, hoodlums, or just like they are living for the devil ---- I would cry out to God, ---- "Why should that person still be having life and my sister gone?" And then I would shed some more tears. I don't say that any more (and God forgive me for ever doing so). Now I find myself being more aware than ever of the Blessings of The Lord. I don't take things for granted. I didn't before, but now, even MORE so. I thank God for the simplest things. Every chance I get to go downtown and walk through our beautiful Circle Centre Mall, I walk and thank God for the ability to do this simple thing. I'm sorry Jenny didn't get a chance to see this mall because----- she would have loved it. ---- She liked nice things.

I do believe ---- and she said this to me also ---- that what she had to go through was to help us not to go through it. Her suffering should alert us to take better care of our bodies, to appreciate good health and physical abilities. And, most of all, ---- to love and appreciate each other, ---- and be grateful to God for the times He gives us together.

Thank God, Jenny is now out of her suffering. Thank God, she is Happy with Him!!

Love you all,
Charlotte

******* * *******

JENNY'S Corner

Yoo Hoo!!

Hey you guys down there. Thought you were rid of me, didn't you? Well, think again! My heart is right there with all of you ---- and I don't want to see any long sad faces. I mean it!

I know Thanksgiving is going to be different this year, but hey, it's going to be all right! You can make it without my "good cooking" (smile), and you all will just have to learn to make my famous fudge cake yourself. Ha! Ha! But seriously, don't grieve for me. I'm having a ball! This Thanksgiving I get to eat all I want and never have to worry about gaining a pound. You all should see my figure now! And Mom, Daddy, Grandma, Granddaddy, Aunt Willa, and all the rest are glad to have me here with them, this year. They all send their love ---- and most of all, Jesus, our Lord and Saviour sends His Love.

So you guys, hang in there! Don't give up. Be encouraged because Jesus is coming back there real soon, and we're coming with Him to get the bodies we left there in the ground, and then we're all going to have a glad reunion as our bodies are changed in the sky and forever be with our Lord and Saviour! And the best part is we'll never be separated again!

I love you all so much --- but you guys know that already!

See you soon,
Jenny

*** ** ***

TWERP'S Corner

Hi, Everybody,

God is so good! In spite of all the devil has thrown at us, we're still going to make it! Praise God!

It is with true joy that I write this newsletter. After the Lord took Cecelia home, I didn't think I'd be able to write an article at all. Then as I lay in bed this morning, thinking of Jenny, as usual. The thoughts just started coming to me of what she might want to say to us. It was so encouraging I had to jump out of bed and write it down before I forgot it. Isn't the Lord good?

I truly thank God for the remaining time He's giving all of us to love, enjoy, and encourage one another. We have to make each day count.

OK, here's what's going on in my life. Oooo-o-o, it's so quiet here it's scary. (smile) My last little Indian on the Totem Pole, Joey, is gone. (Sob, sob) Tears of sadness, or relief? Well, to be honest, a little of both ---- maybe a little more relief. But seriously, Tom and I are enjoying it tremendously. Whoopie!!! Especially the telephone; it has become our friend instead of our tormentor.

Now that the kids are gone, Tom and I are sprucing up our home. Doing some much-needed painting and remodeling. We're truly enjoying it.

Well family, I'm closing now, but let's remember to keep in touch between newsletters. And especially pray for and keep in touch with Poogie and Jenny's kids. If we're missing Jenny this much, ----- quadruple it and imagine what they must be going through ---- especially Poogie.

We all know the Lord, and that it is His will that we encourage one another until He comes.

Maranatha! Look up for our Redeemer is coming quickly!

> I love you all so much!!!
> Jessie Mae

****** * ******

BUTCHIE'S Corner:

Looking forward to hearing from you next time.

*** ** ***

LUCY LOCKETT'S Corner

Missed your "novel" this time. We expect an extra long one next time.

*** ** ***

TWIN #1, LEONARD'S Corner

I am ---- we ALL ---- are believing that we will be blessed with a letter from you next time.

***** ** *****

Those Holland Kids

TWIN #2, LINDA'S Corner

Sorry you didn't get a letter in this time. We know you would have had some beautiful words to say concerning Jenny. Looking forward to hearing from you next time.

***** ** *****

CLOSING WORD

I am BREATHLESS! Wasn't that a wonderful surprise and joy? When I opened Jessie's envelope and saw that letter from Jenny, ---- I could hardly type for my eyes being filled up. It sounded just like her, didn't it? Oh Praise The Lord!! I really needed that! God always comes to our rescue, and He used our dear sister Jessie this time. It's like when I was grieving so badly for my friend Elmira. In my dream the phone rang and it was Elmira. I yelled, "Elmira, is it you? Are you all right?" (I was crying and rejoicing to hear her voice.) She said, with that little laugh in her voice, so typical of her, "Yes, yes, it's me! I'm all right! I'm happy!" It was SO REAL! I awoke, still crying and rejoicing! From that day forth, I stopped grieving for her. So, now, the grieving for Jenny is over! I can think of her with JOY.

Thought I should share Jessie's note to me with you.

Charlotte,

Just wanted to explain Jenny's letter. Monday morning, I woke up with Jenny on my mind (as usual). I was thinking about the newsletter and how empty it was going to seem without Jenny's input. To be honest, I didn't feel like writing anything myself. But as I lay there, Jenny's voice came in my heart, speaking and saying just what I wrote in the letter. I lay there smiling and crying. It was around 5:30 a.m., and it seemed like the Lord was saying, "write it down for the newsletter." I jumped right up and wrote it. Isn't the Lord wonderful?

Every issue someone can write something about her, like an experience, to fill that spot, because, she is still with us, in our hearts.

Jessie

That is a wonderful idea. And thank you, Jessie, for your uplifting letter. I know it was good therapy for me, and I'm sure it was also for the others.

The final word is this. As Jessie said, let's stay IN TOUCH between newsletters. Make use of the good old calendar. Write down when you call each one of your sisters or brothers. We may not be able to travel to each other as we would love to. But we can CALL. We don't have to make it lengthy conversations and cause big phone bills. But if you call one this month, then next month call another. But months and years ought not, and should not, go by without talking with one another.

And let's remember what Cecelia said ---- take care of ourselves. Come on, let's stop the worries, fretting, getting upset, eating improperly, not drinking plenty of water and letting harsh drinks go (or stay to a minimum) like Cokes, etc.. Eat plenty fruit and veggies and grains. And most of all ---- Get PLENTY of Rest ---- Walk and EXERCISE daily. We all are striving to be where Jenny is, but let us go there in God's time, not ours, by rushing it.

Since Marcia has not told us how much the cost will be for the notebooks, I think it would be good to just send her something to get started. Then maybe we can squeeze it out of her exactly how much it cost when she is finished. Thanks, Marcia, for suggesting doing them for Christmas presents. But, with having hours cut and running a home by yourself, I know it can't be too easy. God Bless you for the thought.

I am sending a copy of this newsletter to Chancer, and taking one to Poogie. Yes, by all means, pray for them and Cecelia's other children.

Charlotte

chapter 10

May 1998
Rembering Jenny

"What a wonderful day it is in the month of May." Charlotte feels especially contemplative. "It's been eight months since Jenny died. This is when I would normally be preparing and wrapping her birthday gift; as it is I am putting together our special edition newsletter in her memory."

Charlotte has already received everyone's written statements and she hangs up the phone after taking short verbal additions from each of them. All of her printing tools and writing equipment are spread out in systematic, assembly-line manner on the large pine garden table. The screened-in porch overlooking the back lawn is the perfect spot for an enjoyable project of this sort this time of year.

The morning breeze feels pleasantly relaxing and almost perfect. Occasional wind currents are enough to keep her workspace cool, shaded as it is from the eighty-degree sunshine, but they are too gentle to disturb the colorful stacks of typing paper.

Charlotte hardly notices the dial on the garden clock behind her. When she glances up, she is startled. "Twelve o'clock. My goodness. I've been out here longer than I realized. I'll critique this last draft, fix Jim and me some lunch, then finish preparing these envelopes for mailing."

She gets comfortable on her favorite swinging settee and begins reading.

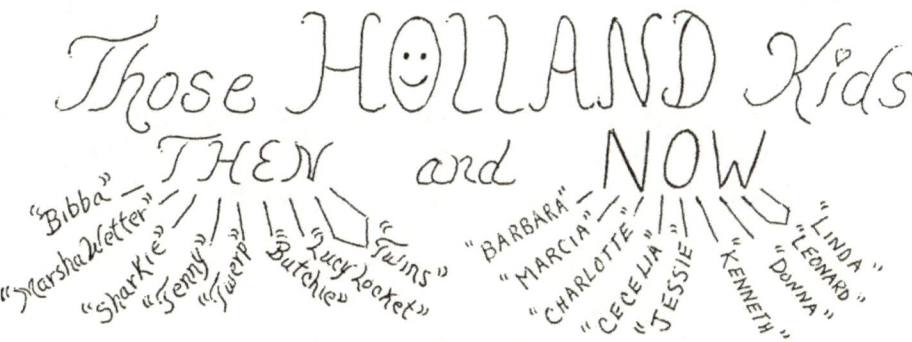

**SPECIAL EDITION
MAY 23, 1998**

"MARCIA *wants to say that* CECELIA HOLLAND *was born May 31, to Kenneth and Idona Holland, in Fort Wayne, Indiana. She was the fourth of 10* children (one, named Marilyn, died at birth). She was a beautiful child: ---- very light complexioned (after Daddy's relatives), with beautiful long and full black hair ----- no hot comb or curlers needed as it was naturally curly. I remember she and cousin-Ruthie (Aunt Willa's daughter) being together in a basket at Grandma's house in the country, and everyone was oohing & aaahing over those beautiful babies.

"Jenny, as we called her when we were all young, was the 'life' of the house at 526 E. Brackenridge Street. She was very 'high spirited' and kept something going all the time. Mother had a difficult time keeping shoes and panties on her, as well as, keeping her hair combed and braided, because Jenny loved to run around 'free as a bird'!

"She was a loving child, but very mischievous. She was always getting a whipping for something. ---- She would yell and scream and beg Mom or Daddy to 'Have Mercy!' ---- but the whippings didn't seem to deter her from getting into something again. When things didn't go her way, or especially when we taunted her by calling her 'Captain Wild Woman,' ---- look out! She would come charging at us, with --- curly hair flying all over her head, and a ---- butcher knife, or whatever she could get a hold of, in hand ---- and chase us all around the house! Our only means of safety was to get to the upstairs front bedroom and lock ourselves in. There we would have to stay, since --- she parked herself outside the door ---- jabbing at the hook-lock with the butcher knife through the crack in the door --- until Mom or Daddy came home, or until we were able to calm her down by promising her something.

"Those were 'close-call' times. --- It's a wonder any of us made it to adulthood. (smile) But when Jenny wasn't acting like 'wild woman' or the 'Bad Sheep' --- she was the 'clown' of the family and kept everyone laughing.

****** ** *******

"BARBARA remembers that... When Jenny became a grown-up, she then became the 'witty' one in the family. She had a comical word for everything that happened. And she could say it in a way to 'crack everyone up.' She could talk about us in a funny way to make us laugh, but if someone else said the same thing --- we would be offended and mad.

"I remember, also, how she would drink coffee and smoke cigarettes when she gained weight after giving birth. She would do this, eating very little food, until she was back at her 'Coca-Cola' figure. I would talk to her about quitting smoking, and give her books to read (about people's lives being changed by Jesus). There was one book that really touched her. It was about a tough girl ----- almost like she was----- whose life had been changed. When Poogie came home off the road, she was telling him about the book; --- I think she wanted him to read it also. I don't know if he actually did or not, but he was interested in what Cecelia was telling him. They were living in a nice apartment (with hardly any furniture in it) at that time. I hope I had some small part in helping to lead her (and Poogie) to Jesus.

"Cecelia took an early disability retirement from Magnavox Company, when her hand was injured. She then began taking Foster Children into her home. Can't remember the exact count, but it was something like nine or ten total. She didn't get to travel very much, which was what she always wanted to do. Her husband was on the road a lot as a truck driver, so she stayed at home with the children. She was a very meticulous housekeeper and an excellent cook. She had dreams of going different places—dreams mostly left unfulfilled. Maybe most of you didn't know this, but she had dreams, also, of having her own auto repair shop. She loved to tinker with mechanical things, and was good at it. So in the meantime, she concentrated on her family, home, church and her God."

"Since we are honoring her, during her birthday month of May: ---- Happy Birthday---- to our beloved sister, Cecelia (Jenny). I do miss her call every day and the way the first thing she would say was, "Whatcha doing?" I also miss her talking about me, when all of us sisters are together. I never got hurt or upset because what she said was so funny.

****** ** *******

"As for me, Charlotte, these are my thoughts and memories of our sis, Cecelia. Jenny was my bad, little sister (two years younger than me.) We all were very close when we were children, but somehow, as we grew into the teen years and older, we seemed to have our own set of friends to run with. Although I loved Jenny just as I loved all my sisters and brothers, somehow we went our separate ways.

"She was sort of on the wild side and always getting in trouble, one way or

Those Holland Kids

another. The only time we seemingly came in contact was to argue and fight when I found out she had gotten into 'my things' and wore a skirt, sweater, blouse or something. Can't remember exactly how old she was at the time when she was sent to Girls' School. I think it was about her early teens, and it was because Mom couldn't do anything with her. I believe Daddy was gone at this time. I remember we all went to visit her at the Girls' School often and she acted so rough and tough, telling us how she and the other girls drank all sorts of stuff to get 'high' on.

"When Jenny was much younger, she and one of the little girls in the neighborhood, ---- Tamala Garfield, were 'two bad peas in a pod.' They both were pretty girls with the same kind of beautiful curly, wild hair. Tamala was killed in an auto accident when she was still a very young pre-teen. We use to say: ----- "Jenny was lucky not to have been with Tamala that night." But we know better now --- it was the Hand of God upon her.

"Cecelia's motherhood life began when she married Chancer and had her firstborn: --- Chancer, Jr. Jessie and I loved that little boy along with our own. Jessie was then married into that family and took Chancer Jr. along, when she went to live in Albuquerque. I went there also for a time with Ritchie, so he and Ritchie grew up together for a while. We all were in Albuquerque only for a short time (we were too homesick), and Chancer Jr. was back with his dear mother, whom he loved. He was a good son to her.

"After that divorce, Cecelia married again and bore five more children. That marriage also ended in divorce. She finally met and married James (Poogie). With this union, she birthed two children ---- Tonya and James, Jr.

"After several years of living the 'worldly' life, of smoking, playing cards, and having some alcoholic drinks, Cecelia and Poogie gave their lives to Jesus Christ. They were filled with the Holy Spirit and became faithful church members.

"We became very close and she wanted Jim and me to come to their house EVERY Thanksgiving, and we did so for many years. We thoroughly enjoyed those DELICIOUS meals!

"Cecelia and I were fellow 'dog lovers!' Once when she, Poogie, Tonya and James came down to Indianapolis, I was astonished that she was the only person (other than Jim and I) who could do anything with our 'crazy' Shepherd, Sheba. Sheba would usually run into her house, ----- if she even THOUGHT you were coming near her. But Cecelia put her on a leash and led her around, teaching her to obey commands. Cecelia said if she could have Sheba a little longer, she would 'break' her completely ---- and I know she could have. I believe she would have been able to get close to Rambo, also, if she was around him more.

"I also, admired how Cecelia decorated and kept her home. Everything had its place --- neatly folded or put away in drawers or where needed. All-in-all, ----- Cecelia and I became great friends as well as sisters, ---- for which I am forever grateful to The Lord!!"

****** ** *******

JESSIE says,

"It's hard to believe that we are almost out of May already. It's even harder to believe that in three more days I will be one year from the big '60'! (Yeow-w-w) But truthfully, that no longer bothers me. For a while I use to look in the mirror and get kind of disgusted at the face of that person staring back at me, and I'd think, 'Who in the world is that?' ....'Oh, that's me.' (smile) It's a shame that Old Father Time keeps messing with folk who aren't doing anything but minding their own business. But God is good, He helps me to look on the bright side ...yep, there is a bright side. I could look like Grandma Moses and feel like her too.

"I'm a little down today. First because I am three days late getting this special newsletter to Charlotte. Second, because I have had to run behind a 3-year-old hyperbol... by the name of Conner, Gayla's little tyke. Really, he's 3 going on 23. (Gayla the second, but in another gender.) Gayla just went back to work, after having a little girl, Kiersten. She was born April fourth, and weighed 6 lbs. 13 ozs. She's a cutie pie.

"The reason I feel down is that I wanted to surprise you all with a pencil sketch of Jenny. I took a picture of her holding James' little boy. She had on her pink housecoat and was grinning so lovingly at him. Oh, how she loved that fat butterball. I worked on that picture for weeks. I could only work on it a little at a time. The snapshot was so small I couldn't get all the details like I wanted. She had her head cocked to one side, and I just couldn't capture her like I wanted to. I just couldn't get her grin. Nobody grins like Jenny! When I looked at her through my magnifying glass she looked so real, like she was getting ready to say, 'Look at Granny's baby...' I miss her so much. Maybe it's for the best. It might be too soon for everyone. I will try again some time.

"There are many things I can say about Jenny. But I will just tell you about two incidents. The first was the time we went to St. Patrick's Catholic School. Cecelia stayed in trouble so much that she kept flunking and ended up in the same grade with me, fifth, I believe. For some reason we had to share the same desk. Jenny was outgoing and impish and I was a little skinny, shy mouse. Our teacher was a Nun named Sister Marie. She was tall and bony and had bucked teeth, and was mean as a whip. It didn't take much for her to sling a book across the room at someone's head or tear hands up with a ruler. I was scared to death of her and she knew it. I tried hard to stay out of her way. The more I tried to stay out of trouble, Jenny would try to get me in trouble.

"One day we were seated together doing our work and Jenny must have gotten bored, so she decided to take her big hips and scoot me right off the seat. On the floor I plopped. When I looked up, there was Miss Bugs Bunny standing over me with her hands on her bony hips, glaring down at me; I wanted to die. Jenny sat there trying to hide her smile and looking like the most angelic being ever. Then she looked down at me as if to say, 'Jessie, whatever are you doing on the floor?' I wanted to clobber her.

"The other time I want to share about was when Jenny came back from Florida last year. I had taken all my crew—I mean kids and grandkids—to Jenny's house to see her. When we arrived, she was on the phone talking to Charlotte. When she came to the door and saw all of us, she said to Charlotte, 'Oh Lord, here's Jessie and she brought her army with her'. She really talked about me. She was pleased that everyone had taken time to come see her. But you all know Jenny, she would keep you laughing.

"We had a great time visiting. When it was time to leave she sat on the couch and said, 'OK, everybody, come and give Aunt Cecelia a big hug and kiss.' You would have thought she was getting ready to pass out $100 bills. I kid you not! Those kids, from the oldest to the youngest got in a single file, which almost reached the door, and anxiously waited their turn to kiss Aunt Cecelia. For some reason, I was trying to get Courtney, Lori's 5-year-old daughter, out of line to do something. She looked up at me with a most serious face, and said, "But Grandma, I'll lose my place in line." I got so tickled. You would have thought Jenny was Santa Claus or something. I'll never forget that. That is one of the memories I will hold dear to my heart. Jenny loved kids and they loved her. She talked rough to them in her way, but they knew she loved them.

"I keep one copy of Jenny's obituary in my bible, one at the head of my bed, and another in a shoebox. When I start feeling sad and I'm missing her a lot, I read the words from the obituary to the family. Then I look at her big, bright beautiful smile and it always helps me feel better. It seems like she is saying those very words to me, personally. You, my family, please read those words; they are beautiful, and I believe they will uplift you."

*** * ***

Donna wants to say...

"Thank the Lord, Cecelia knew her God. Because a year ago in April, she finally went to Indy's I.U. Medical Hospital to have tests run to check out exactly what was happening in her body. For months she thought her problem was a bladder infection and was treating herself accordingly. But things were not getting better; they were getting worse. That was a blow to us all when we heard the dreaded word --- cancer. I'm sure it was a blow also to Cecelia, but outwardly she stood strong. She really was brave. I'm not quite sure I would have been able to stay as calm as she did. "I'm also not quite sure I would have been able to bear the tremendous pain that she experienced. Many times she would just hold her head down, her long beautiful hair falling over her face, and quietly moan, after a painful, long walk from her bed to the bathroom. Then, when she could no longer get up out of bed, she would just cry out whenever a pain hit her--- 'I Love You Jesus!' What a beautiful way to handle pain.

"Melanie, Jessie's daughter, sent copies enough for us all, of the enclosed photos----Thank You, Melanie. The one photo was taken July 4th holiday when Jessie and her whole family went there to see Cecelia. The other photo was taken in late August or early September. That is me in the chair beside her bed. Melanie came over and took the picture. At that time, Cecelia looked extremely thin and gaunt. She asked us to sing some songs. Melanie and I and her girls tried to think of songs to sing. Cecelia sang softly along with us. She was still able to be a little witty----saying, 'All we need is a few more and we will have a nice choir.' The truth of the matter was, we needed a whole LOT more to help us sound like a choir. My voice was screeching and cracking, and ---- I was wishing that Jessie were there to help us out with her wonderful voice.

"Little did we realize --- (Jessie, Charlotte, and I) --- that when we left Cecelia's house in late September, it would be the last time we would see her here on earth. Barbara got to see her a few more times. On Tuesday, September 30, 1997, she left this world to go to that Better Place. She looked nothing like the two photos enclosed, and that as her body lay in the casket, she looked Absolutely

Beautiful. It was as though she had NEVER seen a sick day in her life! It was AMAZING!! Thank God, that is how we are able to get through this, ------ because we do believe that there is a place called Heaven! There is a place where Cecelia is with those other saved loved ones of ours! There is a place where all of them are with our Lord and Savior ---- Jesus Christ! There is a place where we can, and will see her again!"

****** ** ******

CONCERNING FUTURE LETTERS…

I am being impressed to cut down the frequency of our Issues. Everyone does not like to write as often as our newsletter comes out, I feel. Four times a year (every three months) rolls around so quickly. And though it is not too much for some of us, I believe it is for others. No one has said this to me; I just believe this is the way to go. So we can go to three issues per year, every four months (Feb., June, Oct.) or we can have just two Issues per year, (Feb. and Sept. ---- Mother and Daddy's birthday months). Let me know which you prefer. The majority votes win. Will 'Everyone', please let your choice be known. I will let you know the results.

CHARLOTTE

chapter 11

October 2005
Loads of laughter;
extractions from many
letters

Jessie relaxes luxuriantly, enjoying herself in the quiet atmosphere of the back deck. Tom, as usual, has gone over to the church's recreation center. Jessie takes in a deep breath of the crisp morning air with its pungent aftermath of the recently mown lawn. She can always appreciate the many cows that graze endlessly on grass pasturelands receiving the fullness of nutrients found there.

Reclining in her favorite chair she allows the soothing sun's rays to bathe her. "I could lie out here all day," she sighed contentedly. In her position she can maintain a sweeping view of her entire back yard landscape. She admires her handiwork; the fragrant white, yellow, and gold fall blooms lining the perimeter seem to smile back at her. Bold, green, feather-shaped leaves follow the path giving the entire landscape a joyful glow.

"I wish Mom could be here now. She really appreciated pleasantly strong aromas of all kinds. I can almost smell the lemon peels Mom would arrange neatly on the window ledge in the kitchen on Brackenridge Street. As they dried in the sun their delicious smell would become stronger each day. They were much more pleasing to my nostrils during those years than the popular scented candles of today.

"But how well do I know that Mom is in a much better place where she is enjoying the uniqueness of aromas from plants and flowers we will never experience until we join her. I like to remember the mixture of surprise and joy on her face in her casket at the funeral home. That was, of course, until the funeral director turned the corners of her lips down without asking us.

"Mom began to deteriorate after most of us older kids left home. I believe Donna and the twins were still there when she began showing signs of dementia. By the time everyone was gone she had lost her appetite almost completely. We moved her into Barbara's home. Her struggle against heart and lung problems became a losing battle and on a quiet day in September Mom went to sleep with the most beautiful smile on her face, a smile we hadn't seen in a long while. I still miss her as much today as I did in the years soon after her death."

Turning to pick up the familiar large envelope lying next to her, Jessie's thoughts continued. "I truly believe Mom would be thrilled to voice her approval and heart-felt gratitude over our newsletters that have travelled so many miles. These pages of every color in the rainbow have graced the hearts of relatives, friends, and neighbors for many years. The very fact that they began and ended as a tribute to her must certainly bring a bright smile to her face."

Jessie opens the envelope and pulls from it an impressive array of colored pages. "My goodness!" she gasps. "What a striking prism." She takes the time to look a little closer. "There are pages of canary yellow, teal blue, soft purple, sea green, burgundy, pale yellow, steel gray, sky blue, orange, and more. So this is the surprise Charlotte and Donna told us to watch for."

Jessie settles back in anticipation and begins reading.

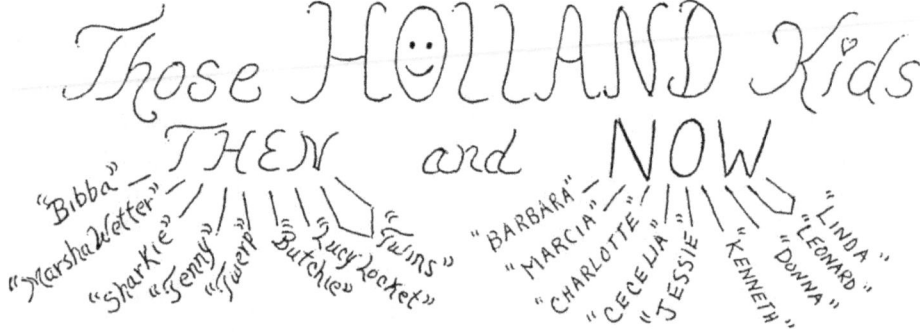

October 30, 2005
A Selection of Letters and Stories

"Hello Sisters and Brothers!

"It's been five years and 24 issues of sharing our thoughts, joys and tears of our childhood years, and of sharing our lives. The peace and harmony we have acquired by keeping in contact with one another is priceless. We have kept this alive, by reminiscing about Mom and Dad's good qualities and the things we loved about them.

"Many of our newsletter readers say that what they enjoyed

the most were the short stories and drawings in many of the issues. We have extracted some of those, which were created specifically with the intention of informing and entertaining, and have grouped them together for you in the form of a large newsletter.

"The biggest surprise and beauty of the following colorful pages, both visibly and heart-felt, is that there are drawings, which were sent in by Kenny and Linda.

"Hallelujah! We never gave up on them,
ENJOY..."

BUTCHIE'S Corner
FEBRUARY 1998

Hi Everyone,

This is your big brother who finally came in from the garage. I put down my tools and have picked up a pen to let you know what I've been up to.

Since retiring from the Air Force in 1980, I've been self-employed with my own auto repair business, and since 1966 I also have had an entertainment business.

KEN HOLLAND
Mechanic

Ken's Mobile Auto Repair
Mechanic • Paint • Body Repair

Tucson, AZ 85730

Vocalist
KEN HOLLAND

Sunset Entertainment
Easy Listening 50's to 90's

Weddings - Private Parties - Bus.

I'm working harder and longer hours now than I did before I retired. I can do just about anything a car might need ----- engine change, major body work, installation of vinyl tops and transmissions, etc. You name it and at a price my customers like. Judy calls me "Super Mechanic."

A friend of ours introduced us to karaoke and that's how I started singing regularly in public. I was in, and won, several contests. Next thing I knew, people wanted to hire me to sing for weddings, private parties, and many different restaurants around town. I usually do most of the jobs myself, but for weddings, I know two girls, both with beautiful voices; one or the other will do the weddings with me so we can sing the duets. That's how I started Sunset Entertainment. I'll tell you more about my shows in future letters.

Since this is my first time writing, I'd like to tell you about my family. I have a wonderful wife, Judy. We have been married for almost 21 years. She keeps me from making the inside of the house look like the garage.

We have three lovely girls, Michelle (26), Jennifer (25), Christina (19), and a son, Darryl (37). Darryl worked for IBM for years and took classes to get his degree from college. He now works for the State as a computer programmer. He bought a beautiful home and is still looking for "Miss Right."

I have five wonderful and very active grandchildren:

Grandchildren	Parents
Brandon 6 yrs	Jennifer & David
Alyssa 5 yrs	(Married 6 years)
Mayloni 4 yrs	Michelle & Tim
Kyana 3 yrs	(Married 7 years)
Rashon 2 yrs	Christina's son, an upcoming "Basketball Star"

Rashon is only 2, but he amazes people with his ability to dribble, shoot and make baskets. Move over, Michael Jordan!

As you all probably remember, I loved to go to the movies when I was a kid. The problem was you could watch the movie over and over with no extra charge. I remember telling myself I would just watch it once and get home so Mother wouldn't find out. But it's hard to leave a movie like King Kong. Next thing I knew, the theater was closing and it was dark. I tried to sneak in the upstairs window over the kitchen at home. It had worked a few times in the past, but this time Mother was waiting with a stick. Mother made her point ---- I never did that again.

Sorry it took me so long to write. I'm going to try and do better this year. I have enjoyed reading all of your letters, and am looking forward to the next one. I Love You All.

Your Loving Brother,
Kenny

******* ** ********

LUCY LOCKETT'S corner
FEBRUARY 1998

Hello! Hello! Hello!
Blessings to all! My apologies for being absent from our last newsletter. I am

hopeful this one finds each of you, my Dear Sisters and Brothers, encouraged and blessed.

    I am still mourning somewhat, because I keep taking Cecelia's funeral announcement out and looking at her picture and every now and then I cry a little for brief moments. I really miss her a lot! However, the Lord is blessing, and I have a small testimony. Strange things are happening!! I think the Lord is healing me. When I look at the evidence: -----

(1) I feel Great!! Not completely well, but ----- really good. This even in the midst of Christmas and New Year's festivities when I sneaked a piece of German Chocolate cake Deanna made, when she wasn't looking.

(2) Also, I'm not having any pain where I normally do. Praise The Lord!! And you know, I'm not real certain when it went away. One day I just noticed that it was gone and was very surprised ----- even a little suspicious. After all, being in chronic constant pain, for 3 and 1/2 years, you can understand why I had to be certain it was really gone.

    Best of all, I am gaining weight. I'm not sure exactly how much, because I "sort of" gave my scale away, out of frustration a while ago. But I am able to wear clothes that were way too large last year. And when I happen to walk past a mirror, I have to go back and look again.

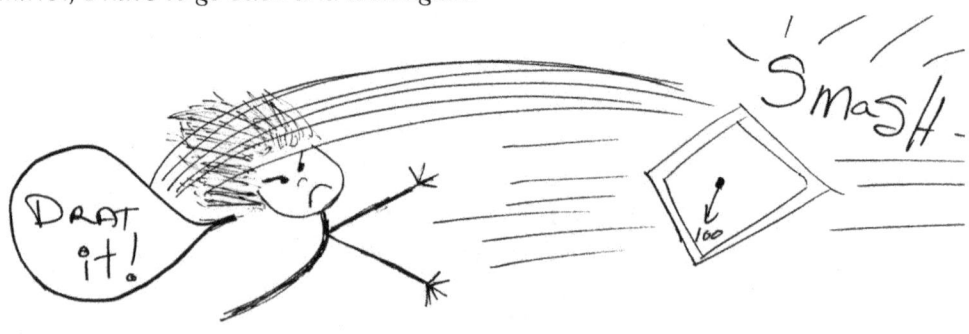

LUCY LOCKET
FEBRUARY 1998, continued

Charlotte, I hope this big fat package (newsletter issue) didn't frighten you, when it arrived. I'm glad I called you first to soften the shock!

Barbara, it was really fun to spend some time with you. It's always a treat when we sisters get together, although I enjoy it more when we sit around with our feet propped up reveling in the "Word" with our Hot Cups Steaming!

Linda,
We all know what a "computer whiz" you are, therefore you had no excuse for not getting your letter ready.
So, I'm on my way over right now to 'Beat you with a Wet Noodle' ----- So LOOK OUT!!

LUCY LOCKET'S CORNER
MAY 1998

I may have a get-together here in my ONE ROOM ABODE pretty soon, and everyone likes the healing foods that I serve. Can you just imagine how this will go over? The owner of the house, where I'm renting a room will think I've FLIPPED MY LID.

Those Holland Kids

Well, on May 31st, Cecelia would be 61 years old, and I would be picking out her card right about now. I really miss her. I like to remember her in the years following 1967 when she drank coffee non-stop, and would always eat lots of dry toast with it, to keep her weight down. I used to follow her and Poogie around because I thought he was going to hurt her during their arguments. Now that I think about it, ----- that was pretty silly of me. (smile)

CONTINUED,,,,
Some of you may be wondering what happened to the Health News I promised ----- well, got an upgraded computer, but didn't realize my brain needed upgrading as well, to get around in all the high-tech software. So off to computer school I must go, else I wasted my money. I hope to enroll this month. It was hilarious to watch me go from intelligently communicating the purchase of the computer, to "duh" when sitting down to create my newsletter.

So give me another month or so, and it may be at your door!!
Looking forward to seeing you Hoosiers in July!

So Long Ladies,
So Long Kenny,
Hello Leonard & Linda,
Love, your Sis,
Donna

*** * ***

LUCY LOCKET'S Corner
SEPTEMBER 1998

I know this issue is supposed to be dedicated to Daddy but I don't remember anything about him. Barbara and I calculated once and found that I was about 1 year old when Daddy went into the hospital; I missed knowing him. Jessie, your box arrived and was here when I returned, and I've been dancing around it ever since. I've been waiting for just the right moment to open it. When I finally did, I was pleasantly surprised. The portrait is a magnificent work of art. Mom looked so pretty and serene; Daddy looked so very handsome. And Jessie Girl, you are so good, I have all confident that you will conquer that masterpiece of Cecelia's before long. My portrait gallery collection is now 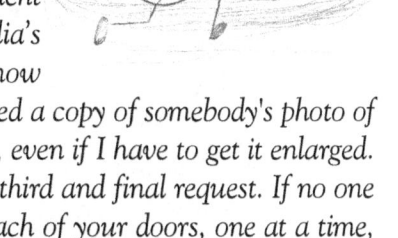 complete except for one of Cecelia; I really do need a copy of somebody's photo of her. Please! Please! Somebody send me a picture, even if I have to get it enlarged. I promise to send it right back to you. This is my third and final request. If no one responds this time, I will physically show up at each of your doors, one at a time, and hang around in your house until you have convinced me you're clean and don't have one (smile).

TWERP'S corner
FEBRUARY 1999

Hi Family!
Does anyone know what it's like after a tornado or hurricane sweeps through your house? The awe you feel as you look around and realize you survived? Well, sisters and brothers, that's exactly how I feel! Truly, truly blessed!!! I'm talking

about that crazy flu that's been going around. It got hold of me the second of February and today, March first, I feel like a new person. I've never been knocked down this long since I had that gosh awful ear surgery a few years back. I truly praise God for bringing me through this nightmare.

It all happened Monday night, Feb. first when my neighbor called me crying and barely able to talk. She needed me to come and pray for her. I grabbed my coat and as I was heading next door I breathed a prayer that God would be with me and use me. She was in bad shape. She was crying and gasping for air, and hardly able to breathe. She has a history of bronchitis. After much prayer, she finally calmed down and her breathing returned to normal.

She later found out that she had a bronchial infection and that crazy flu. The next day I started getting a tickle in my throat. I thought, "Oh no, I bind this." But by that evening I had to cancel my teacher's meeting because I was feeling so bad. I was zonked out for the next few days. I had no appetite and was very listless. Sunday morning, I was feeling somewhat better and decided to venture out to church. Not a good move! Especially since that Saturday Jim (Charlotte's husband) came by to see about his little sis. He sat right at my table and warned me not to get out too soon because a relapse would wipe me out.

Was he ever right! The only thing he left out was the tornado and the hurricane. (smile) That Sunday was cold, windy and rainy. The next day was when I heard the whistle of the train. The coughing got so bad I could barely talk without a coughing spell. I had to sit up at night because lying down made it worse. I stayed in until Thursday when I finally went to the doctor. I was diagnosed with an acute bronchial infection and put on sulpha antibiotics. I was warned to take the medication for the full 10 days, twice a day. It did help control the coughing and cleared up the yellow phlegm but my little frail body couldn't tolerate that sulpha. I haven't had a licking like that since Mom held me by my little bony arm and wore my little bitty legs out. (smile)

My appetite was already pitiful and that drug took the rest of it. It kept a horrible taste in my mouth. Absolutely, nothing tasted good. Not even pizza, my favorite. The pounds rolled off of me. All I could do, from day to day, was go from bed to chair to couch and then back to bed. I staggered like a drunkard, when I walked. Tom wanted to take me to the hospital but I insisted I would be all right, once I finished taking the pills.

Charlotte and Jim found out I was sick. They were upset because I didn't let them know. I had to confess I was afraid to let Jim know that I ignored his warning. He did wait until I was feeling better before he let me have it.

Wednesday the 17th, Tom went to teach Bible Class. I was in bed feeling weak and washed out when Barb and Charlotte called me, very concerned about my staying on that medication. They didn't have to twist my arm. They prayed for me and my mind was made up to stop taking it. The next morning I skipped my dose and started feeling better immediately. Charlotte called the next day checking on me, noticed the cough still there and that evening, after working late at the Cookie Store, showed up at my door loaded with vitamins and herbs for me and a very good health book.

I told Tom later, that Charlotte & Jim are "Love in Action." They have no idea what that meant to me. I kid you not. Those vitamins & herbs are GREAT! And then to top it off, the next day Charlotte came over with Skyscraper Ron, (Barb's son). He's so tall he looks like his head will hit my ceiling. Ron moved to Indianapolis, which I'm sure Barb will tell you all about it. Anyway, Charlotte brought me two more bottles of health aids: Echinacea and Goldenseal for colds and Acidophilus to get my strength back. The first time I took them I could tell the difference. We were sitting on my couch and I'm thinking about how much she must have paid for all this. These things are expensive. Nonchalantly I asked, "How much did these cost?" Her eyes widened as they pierced into mine. "Why?" she wanted to know. "Just wondering," I casually remarked, hoping she would not see through me. All I need is to find a way to repay her.

Sunday the 21st, I wasn't able to go to church because of weakness in my limbs. I was beginning to

feel very lonely. When Tom came home he had a huge, beautiful planter from the church. He also had a card with everyone's signature and words of encouragement. There was a card from the choir with signatures, and a love offering collected from the church. All I could do was cry. God is so good. The church had slacked off calling me because of my coughing spells. But they were praying for me and sending me cards. I even got a card from Sheba and Ricky (Charlotte and Jim's babies). It was a dog in a doghouse with a water bottle on his head saying he hoped I would get better so I could come out to play. How cute!

"All things work together for good to them who love the Lord." That is so true. The Lord dealt with me on many things, while I was still. He restored my joy that had left a while back. He allowed me to see so much love in action. And my neighbor, who is back to work, is excited about getting a recommended book on nutrition and starting on her vitamins and herbs. I believe this is God's way of giving her total healing. Isn't God good?

Do you all remember me asking in my last letter if anyone had been in a tornado and survived? I ask you another question. Has anyone ever been on a ground roller- coaster? Well, I have. I made the mistake of getting into my daughter Leslie's car to take her daughter, Michelle, to the airport. The plane was to leave for California at 9:55 p.m. What time do you think she came to pick me up? Why, 9:25 p.m. Now, anyone in their right mind would have bowed out gracefully and said, "You go ahead, sweetheart. I'll say my goodbye here." But, oh no, not Jessie Mae! She climbs into the car... buckles up... and Lord have mercy... the roller-coaster ride begins.

I kid you not, that little gal was driving like a speed demon. It seemed like we were taking the curves on two wheels. She weaved in and out between cars and semi's like they weren't even there. I was pressing the floorboard so hard I'm sure

there's a dent in it. I cautioned her to slow down, which she did for a second or two, then back to the whiplash.

Would you believe, after all that, the plane was delayed, almost an hour. I prayed on the way, "Lord, please hold that plane." My mistake was not sharing my prayer with Leslie. Then she could have slowed down, and I could have enjoyed the ride. I told her, and meant every word, that I would never in this lifetime ride with her again, if she was late for something. She just laughed.

LUCY LOCKET'S Corner
JULY 1999

Well, on the lighter side, I've been spending time getting organized for greater efficiency of time and energy. I'm not yet settled from the move, due to too much stuff and no place seemingly to put it. So I'm being blessed with the expertise of a sweet little Taiwanese, born-again Christian girl named Thia, who has a ministry and business of organization consulting. She is working with me using a filing system called 'Genesis'. After three hours in my little office, I was amazed to see what we had accomplished. I now have the foresight to see how much precious time will be saved when we finally complete our work together.

My greatest problem of course is trashing unnecessary items. She (Thia) made the statement in the beginning that she will never throw anything away without approval. So when we find something like a uniquely made screw in the wrong place I must decide to toss it or put it in a categorized pile. Thia showed me a staple remover that wasn't working properly. (Oh well, let's call a spade a spade—it was

broke). She said very softly, as we sat on the floor in the midst of our accumulations, "Can we toss this? You have two others and it's broken—SEE?"

Now in the natural realm, one thing was happening, but in the spiritual realm, something totally different was going on.

So you see there is a deliverance associated with her ministry; I am getting uncluttered. It's no wonder she chooses to begin each work session with prayer.

I was just thinking ---- (a dangerous pastime of mine, you know). What if this leftover fatigue I've been suffering from, for some time now, is my THORN IN THE FLESH? Knowing my old self, with all of the energy I used to have, by now I would be halfway up some small mountain, as my current exercise quest.

Barbara and George just left heading for Kentucky; I really enjoyed them. The extremely hot weather slowed us down a little and kept us from any attempts at sightseeing. My great plans, to have a small feast prepared, went belly up so we ate out a lot. When Charlotte comes in October, I will have planned more wisely, so that we can enjoy each other with feet resting on cushions, our teacups in hand, and all we'll need to do is make short trips to the kitchen. I plan on having millet/corn stuffing in Cornish hen, rutabaga/Brussels sprout/sweet onion medley, sweet potato pie and cucumber wakame (ocean vegetable) salad. Sound wonderful? But, of course, if all flops, ---- we'll be eating out of a pizza box.

Barbara, just wanted you to know that what we thought was a sty on my eye may have been an insect bite. One of my clients and I were evaluating it and he said it appeared to be a spider sting. I decided to go on a short all-juice fast for two days and it was drying up and getting much smaller; I know you were concerned because it was pretty ugly.

Don't know what it is with this left eye of mine since this is the third attack. I just may fast on fresh juices one day a week to prevent any further problems because it's obviously very effective. I seem to have more energy now. And who knows? Maybe I'll grow up to be like you. You, who has so much of it, that your coffee hour is the wake-up call to the birds in the neighborhood.

Just kidding!

Jessie, hope you are staying well. In the future just keep your distance from sick neighbors who call on your blessings. It's acceptable, you know, to shout your words of encouragement and healing over the fence, as you send her a nice gesture of beautiful flowers. (smile)

Those Holland Kids

TWERP'S Corner
NOVEMBER 1999

I started to read the newsletter last night, but Tom had gone to bed early with a headache, so I reasoned I'd better wait because it is so hard for me to laugh quietly. Oh-h-h, I'm so glad I waited. It was hilarious. I laughed so long and so hard and loud, I was expecting someone to come banging on my door to see if I was all right. I kid you not! I guess the only ones who heard me were the pigeons, squirrels, and cats outside.

Oh, family, I love you all so much! Just reading your letters fills my heart to overflowing. I already e-mailed Leonard my thanks and praises on his wonderful letter. I told him, "Look at what you have deprived the family of." (smile)

I have two incidents I want to tell you all about. I hope it won't take up too much space. The first is about Conner, Gayla's grown 4-year-old son. Michelle, Leslie's 9-year-old daughter was getting baptized last month at our church. As she was preparing for it, Conner was with me and stated, "I want to get baptized." I told him he had to wait until he was older. He wouldn't be put off and kept pressing me. I finally told him that only people who had accepted Christ in their lives could get baptized. I asked him if he had accepted Christ. He said, "Yes, I did that a long time ago." Me and the lady who was with me cracked up. We both agreed we couldn't say anything against that. So, that little fellow was baptized.

After the baptism, we had Holy Communion. I explained to Conner the meaning. When I mentioned the crackers, his eyes lit up. As the tray was held out to him, I told him to get just one of the small pieces of cracker. Afterwards he said, "I wanted the big square crackers." I guess he was hungry. He's a mess! Gayla has really got her hands full with that lil' guy.

This next incident is about myself. It happened at me and Tom's 15th Pastor and Wife's Anniversary, this past Sept. We were sitting up in front of the church in these lovely chairs while a guest Pastor was preaching.

All during service my slip needed adjusting. I couldn't find the appropriate time to get up and go to the restroom to fix it. I already felt like a fish in a fishbowl.

When the minister gave the benediction I took the opportunity and dashed to the restroom right behind our chairs. This restroom was situated next to the choir stand and baptismal.

As I got to the door, someone was already in there. I knew I had to hurry and get back so I ducked into the door leading to the baptismal. I locked it in case a visitor accidentally opened it.

After I made my adjustments, I unlocked the door.... turned the knob...but it wouldn't open. I tried again and again, but that door wouldn't budge.

I wanted to panic! My mind started racing. "What am I going to do?" All I could think of was poking my head over the baptismal glass, waving and saying, "Help! I'm locked in!" That would have been a sight! Me and this Big gold hat rising up out of the baptismal, scaring everyone half to death, or either everyone rolling on the floor with laughter.

After canning that idea, I said, "Lord, Help me!" ...and guess what? When I turned the knob again, the door came right open, just like that! God is so good! He also has a sense of humor. so long for now. Love always, Your Sis, Jessie.

LUCY LOCKET'S Corner
NOVEMBER 1999

I thoroughly enjoyed Charlotte and Jessie. We had a wonderful time of relaxation, fellowship and food. I love the way Charlotte has those conversations with the television programs. She was having such a grand ole' time that we would have delayed her trip home, except Jessie wasn't really crazy about our city's traffic. I can't say that I blame her; it is pretty bad.

SHARKIE'S Corner
March 2000

Ricky, MY LITTLE 4-LEGGED MONSTER, is still trying to "run the house." I am really getting "sick of this bad booger." I told Jim, "We are too old for this dog!" He barks about everything ------ I can't move freely around my own house without him growling and barking. And when either of us gets ready to leave ---- he REALLY "cut Jack!" I would like to give him to someone ---- but I'm afraid because that person might not be able to put up with his behavior and hurt or kill him. So ---- I guess I'm stuck with him.

Sheba is still a sweet dog; however, she still comes out of her house at night and howls like a wolf, when we are trying to sleep. (she really does have some wolf in her.

Looking forward to "getting together" with you sisters soon!
Love,
Charlotte

TWERP'S Corner
MARCH 2000

In remembrance of Mama, you all recall how she was so talented with her hands at sewing. She did excellent work and was always at the sewing machine, creating lovely outfits for her children. I remember especially the little red velvet skirt and cape she made for me. I was around 7 or 8. Remember when capes were in? I was so proud of that outfit. Mom and I were in the upstairs, front bedroom. I wanted all of the world to see my lovely outfit. So I decided to hang out of the window, holding my skirt and cape.

I began yelling to everyone within hearing range, "Look everybody. See my pretty skirt and cape Mama made me!" Mom sat and smiled proudly and lovingly scolded me.
"Now, Jessie, come out of that window and be quiet."
I thought it was pretty neat to be able to share with the world the little happenings in our little abode at 526 E. Brackenridge Street. So when I found a strand of Mom's gray hair, I immediately hung out of the window again, this time waving the gray hair. I excitedly shouted my enthusiasm to the world, "Hey, look, everybody here's Mama's gray hair!" This time Mom's Smug smile took a U-turn. "Girl, get out of that window, NOW!" as she gave my Little boney frame a Helping hand.
Ah-h-h kids ! ! !

I also remember when I used to be terrified of the upstairs bedroom closet. The one in our bedroom was more like an attic for storage than anything. It didn't have a regular lock. It was a block of wood on a nail, and we had to turn the block to keep the door shut. Remember guys? I don't know why I was so afraid.

It was probably from all of you guys telling me stories of the boogie man hiding in there and waiting to come out and get me. I know Cecelia got a kick out of scaring me. I was so gullible. No one could pay me to go into that closet. Whenever I was up there alone, you'd better be sure that I always kept one eye on that door, and the other eye on that block of wood that had to be in the right place.

LUCY LOCKETT'S CORNER
MARCH 2000

Hi everyone!!!

It's time once again to chat.

It's time also for our annual sister's reunion. We've been discussing the month of July, so that we can also be here with cousin Pearl, for the family reunion as well. If Atlanta is really the choice and you gals put me in charge of our activities----Look Out!!---- and start taking your 'vita tabs' right now. This time, reverse psychology is in the making and instead of planning to kick back and get our beauty rest, we will 'PLAN FOR' kicking up our heals; So bring your tennis shoes. Guess you'll also need to bring a rope so we can hog-tie Barbara and drag her behind us, as she kicks and screams to stay home and go to bed (smile)

TWIN # 2's CORNER
MARCH 2000

Oh yes! If any of you know any atheists, send them to spend a day with Donna and she'll prove to them that there really is a God, especially if they ride in the car with her! They will Worship God and be the Holiest and Most Faithful Christians on earth. They will know there has to be a God that drives that car for Donna! (Smile) Here is an example of Donna driving.

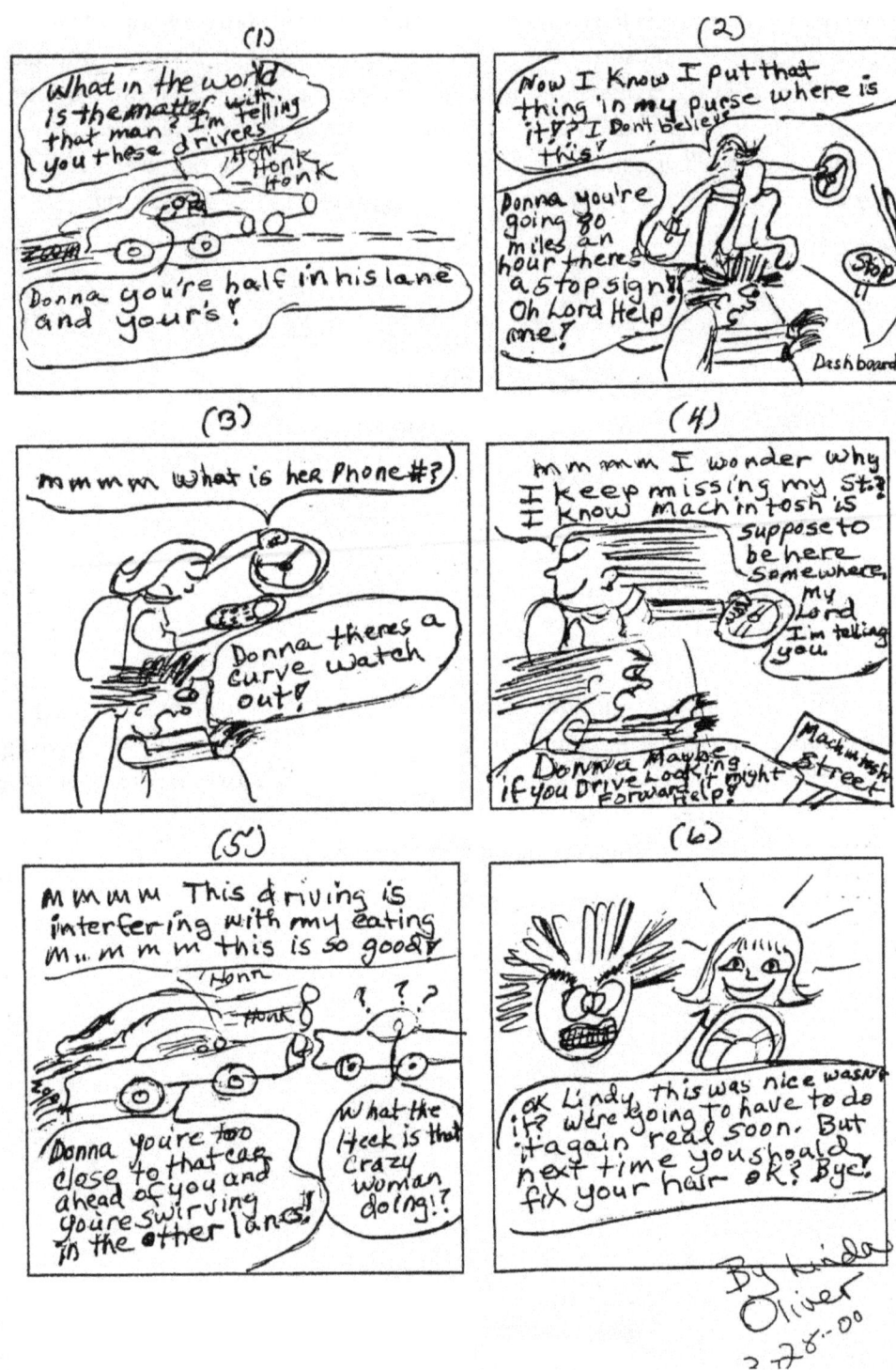

TWERP'S Corner
JULY 2000

My time is not my own these days since Gayla moved to Atlanta. She moved the first of June and is staying with Rhonda until she is able to get her own place. I've been keeping Conner, her 5 year old. He's five with the mind of a 20 year old. Seriously! He's something else. Lovable, but still a handful! When he gets bored he entertains himself by hiding our cordless phone. You should see me playing hide & seek trying to distinguish where the handset locater ringing is coming from. I narrowed it down to the dining room.

There's not that many places it could be. I finally found it in the bottom of the china cabinet, behind the glass doors, pushed way under all the linen tablecloths. I could have clobbered him.

One morning I asked him how many eggs he wanted for breakfast. He looked at me with his great big eyes. With his arms encircling his head, he looked up at the ceiling, as if deep in thought. He thought and thought. Finally, he said, "How about 11?"

I just celebrated my 61st birthday on May 23rd. I figured, just because I'm getting older, doesn't mean I can't try to keep up with the times. So I decided to get a facial, and get rid of all this excess hair on my face.

At my beautician, there is this little oriental lady who does facials. She uses a straight razor to arch eyebrows and take off the hair. She's really good.

As soon as I sat in the chair she laid me back, took one look at me and said, "Ooh Mah Gahd!" "Dis is talible!" "Wook at all dis haah!" With every stroke, she repeated over and over, "How talible!" Then she proceed to hold up her hand with all the shavings in it to show all the other operators and clients. I felt like the Ape Woman. She shaved my hairline, my eyebrows, you name it, she shaved it. As she progressed, periodically, she showed me gruesome shavings. "Wook!" she said with delight. Then she decided to go to each operator and "Show & Tell. "Hav you evah seen any thing lak dis?"

When she was almost done she changed her song. "Ooh-h-h, you ah beautiful" "You wook lak a movie stah." On and on she went, which seemed like an eternity. I thought she'd never shut up. When she handed me the mirror, I was half expecting to see a transformed vision of loveliness. What a let down when I gazed into the mirror and all I saw was Jessie with a brighter, cleaner looking face with arched eyebrows. Oh well, so much for "A Day At The Beauty Parlor."

Before I close, I have to tell you about Joey's iguana, Iggy. Personally, I really care for the little critter. If it wasn't for me, the poor thing would starve. Joey is gone more than he's home. He knows I'll feed him. Yes, I'll feed him, but I do not pick him up. I can't stand his long claws.

While we were in Ft. Wayne, Iggy got out of his cage. Probably searching for food. Conner saw him perched on the back of the couch in the den. He had gotten out before and I had to put on Tom's huge winter glove to catch him. I tiptoed toward him with his dish of romaine lettuce. He immediately started gobbling it. He was starving.

As he was eating, I was trying to boost my nerves. After a while he must have sensed that something funny was going on, or maybe he felt my perspiration splattering on him or maybe the loud knocking of my knees gave him a clue. For he stopped eating...looked up... cocked his head to one side. I knew it was now or never. I felt he was getting ready to make a wild dash for safety..... Whop!.... Down came that huge glove. I thought he was going to have a heart attack, the way he wiggled. I almost had one myself as I felt those long claws all the way impulse to drop him. Squealing, (me.... not Iggy) I flew and dropped him in his cage. I slammed the door. I was literally a nervous wreck. Kids.... Critters!!! Lord help me!

On that note, I'll say o long for now. I love you all so very much. May The Lord continue to bless and keep you all.

Love!
Always,
Your Sis.
Jessie

LUCY LOCKET'S Corner
JULY 2000

Jessie, I liked your article in the last newsletter about the bedroom closet that had you spooked. It reminded me about how the basement in our house gave me nightmares. I will never forget how petrified I always was whenever all of you girls were gone from home and I was left alone with that basement door. The worse part of it was that I had to pass by it, back and forth, to the kitchen and bathroom. I don't remember why I had such a terrible problem about it; maybe some of you know. All I know is that there was something very eerie about it. No one could convince me that there weren't ugly trolls living down those stairs.

It seems that the broom or mop was kept down there and I agonized at the thought of retrieving them. Oh! The good old days.

Linda, why are you such a big Show off? I heard you had your article for this issue turned in two months ago. It's now 1:00 a.m. and I have 2 days to get it into Charlotte's mailbox. Of course I only started on it a couple of hours ago. But you are still a big 'Ham'.

See you all at the reunion!

Those Holland Kids

TWERP'S Corner
FEBRUARY 2001

SPEAKING OF GRANDCHILDREN,,,,,,,,,,,,

Leslie, my daughter, shared this with me. They were at home. Jeffrey (AGE 3) was sitting on his bed playing with his toys and Jalen (AGE 4), being a bug, as usual, started picking with Jeff. They started arguing and Jeff got mad and said, "Shut up, Jalen!" Jalen said, "Who's Jalen?" Jeff said, "Ah Jalen, you know who you are, you're just trying to be stupid!" Jalen said, "Stupid? What does stupid mean?" By now Jeffrey was so upset he was practically in tears. He yelled and said, "Jalen, you are getting on my nerves!" Jalen: "Nerves? What is nerves?"

Jeff: "You better stop copying off me!!!" Jalen: "What does stop copying off me mean?" By this time Leslie was in her bedroom laughing so hard she could hardly control herself. Jalen just carried it on and on. Poor Jeff was a basket case because he kept falling right into Jalen's trap. Leslie was finally able to tell Jalen to cut it out.

I cracked up, when she told me this. I could just see Little Jalen, with his little impish eyes and grin. I kid you not! he's no more than two feet tall. He doesn't have hardly any legs. His head is the biggest thing about him. Tom calls him and Jeff, "The Buckets."

Tom gave me a pair of boots for Christmas. They were real nice boots. The only problem was when I tried them on, my legs looked like broomsticks in 5 gallon buckets. This will never do, I thought. So off shopping I went in search of a pair of boots that looked half way decent on me. One pair I tried on fit me ok, but the heels and soles were so thick that I looked like a skinny version of wonder woman. Next I tried on an ankle high boot which is the fashion now. Oh my, they made me look like a creature from outer space. What ever happened to plain old boots of yesteryears? Cousin Karen, do you design shoes? If you do, please keep your skinny-legged cousin

in mind. (smile)

Oh, oh, I've gone over into another page. But I have to share this: Kids these days, are so intelligent. My neighbor's 5-year-old granddaughter, Tamiren, challenged me to a game of Uno. I hadn't played that game in years but I figured, what the heck, she's only 5 years old. Her mom told me that Tamiren was a whiz at the game. I wasn't doing anything else, so I decided to humor her. Big, big mistake! That little kid was tough. Just when I thought I had the game and was ready to shout, 'Uno', she would wham a big 'Draw Four' on me. After 15 minutes or so, I felt this was getting ridiculous! "Jessie," I thought to myself, "Get this over with. Enough is enough!" "You would have thought I'd take pity on her because she was a kid, but this was no ordinary kid...! She sat across from me, cool as a cucumber, with a big grin on her face and a glint in her eyes, as she bombarded me with Wild Cards, Draw Twos, Draw Fours, and Reverses. I sat there trying to look calm, but I was sweating. After a grueling 30 minutes I shouted "UNO!" and won! Wow! Tamiren quietly collected all the cards and challenged me to a game of Concentration, which I foolishly accepted, reveling in my victory. She proceeded to whip my socks off, game after game after game. Oh well, you can't win them all!

After the game she looked me in the face and began studying me closely. Finally, she said, "Why is your hair different colors? Black...white.... brown, or is it orange?" She stood there a few inches from my face, awaiting an answer, with a solemn, quizzical look on her face. How do you explain to a 5 year old that Miss Clairol was loosing her touch with my hair? All I could do, at that point was shrug and return her wide-eyed stare. That's the third time that little woman, in a kid's body, had me sweating. I should have run it down to her. She probably would have said, "Oh, ok! I understand! Get with it, Miss Jessie!"

Well, family, I'm closing for now. Hope this finds everyone doing well and prospering. God bless you all! I love you so much!

Until next time,
Love,
Jessie Mae

LUCY LOCKET'S CORNER
FEBRUARY 2001

Hello ladies!

For once I am completely speechless; I can think of nothing to elaborate upon. Have been sitting with a pad and a pen for days and my mind is not coming up with a thing. No little jokes, no pictures, no funny stories ---- NOTHING!!
Sorry Jessie.

The thing I will say is that the sister reunion was great as usual. As always, I enjoyed soaking up all of your spiritual wisdom. And I always learn something new. All in all, it is just very comforting being together, almost like old, old, old times in shall we say old, old, old bodies (smile). You all are such gracious guests. Wish I had a tape recorder going so we could play back your Ooooh, Ooooh's and Mmmmmm's when you came into the kitchen in the mornings. Breakfast has always been my favorite meal of the day. My preference is Belgian waffles, potatoes with onions and lots and lots of green tea.

Jessie and Marcia certainly know How to relax. Whenever they came up missing and we wondered where they were, Jessie could usually be found either napping or with Marcia in the garden reading and doing giant cryptograms.

Marcia would sit for hours until we felt we needed to check on her to see if she was still breathing. I'm trying my very best to be like you two. I keep my puzzle books next to my bed but don't ever pick them up.

It was so funny I had to chuckle the time Barb and I was peering out of the patio window, as we were trying to figure what Charlotte, Marcia and Jessie were actually doing. We eventually realized that they were asleep.

Well, some of you are probably wondering what's the 'Big Foot' in all of the cartoons. Tues. Nov. 28th started out to be a great day and what I planned to be the start of a new and exciting agenda. Projects were under control and I was feeling a little free. Had gone to the gym that morning and worked out on the treadmill and weights. Also was committed to make it a practice,

at least 2 times a week. That devilish little plant that sits on my frig, the one that 'USED TO' get my tender loving care, 'MAY NOT' get any more. (smile) It had been pleading to me all day to give it some water. All the other plants were as happy as could be. After coming home and feeling quite pleased with the day, I decided to finally give it a real good watering. I thought I would take a short-cut by using the stool that sits next to the island. The rest is history. As I stepped down the stool slipped on the rug and my foot flew out from behind me. My head hit the corner of the island on the way down. I can be thankful though that I came out of it with only a very temporary black eye and 2 hairline-fractures on my foot. The doctor put me in a boot-type cast that is causing me lots of problems. I had been driving myself around but now it's back to bed and off my feet again. Now, that was 2 weeks ago and I have totally forgotten (or blocked out, more than likely) plants and water. And today I am watering only those I can reach comfortably. And I think I am detecting vibrations of a little attitude coming from the refrigerator (smile). Come to think of it, the poor thing hasn't had a drink since that fateful day, Oh well, it will survive.

Linda came by, one day, to see how I was getting along and she was dressed up so sharp, I can't believe I didn't grab my camera and snap a picture. She looked like Essence Magazine. She had on a tan 2-piece outfit, with a black jacket and shoes, and her beeper was attached to her belt. I said, "go on girl"! Of course, there I stood looking like 'Aunt Jenoonie' as Cecelia used to say.

TWERP'S Corner
AUGUST 2001

Charlotte, I want to put your mind at ease. Your case of computeritis is not uncommon. I was discussing your lack of interest for the computer with Gayla the other day, The Lord took me back to the hard time I had adjusting to mine. Before I got mine, I had never touched a computer, or a mouse. Everything was so alien and complicated, I was tempted many times to tell Tom to take it back to the store. Seriously, I didn't think I'd ever catch on. But Pat, from church, kept encouraging me. When she told me that one day, I'd be an old hand at it, I thought, "Right!" As I learned, my calls for help became fewer. Pat said she was glad I was learning, but also saddened because I didn't need her as much. So Charlotte, I'm not disappointed. I fully understand. One day you'll wonder, as I do now, how you ever got along without one. (smile)

...Let's see, What else has been going on???? Oh yes, I celebrated my big "62nd" Birthday. It was real nice and quiet. AH-H-H! And guess what? I worked on my jig-saw puzzle. I got all the edges together. Unfortunately, that's as far as I got. I haven't gotten back to it since May. Sad! Huh? On that day I had some great excitement. I almost had to call the fire dept....... No, the candles on my cake wasn't burning. (smile) I put some oil in the skillet and unwittingly went upstairs to do something. I forgot all about the skillet until I saw smoke curling up the stairs.

Before I could get down there the smoke alarms were blasting like crazy.

And there I was scurrying around opening the doors and windows to let the dark clouds of smoke out. It was so bad I had to sit out on the porch, trying to act nonchalant, but looking really silly with all that smoke billowing out the doors and windows. My, my! What we old folks won't do for a little excitement!

LUCY LOCKET'S CORNER
AUGUST 2001

Hi there you absolute strangers!
Where have you been, and why have you taken so long pulling this newsletter together? You ought to be ashamed of yourselves keeping everyone waiting. I know how ungodly busy you are but that is NO EXCUSE. I expect everyone of you to get your act straightened up and -------------

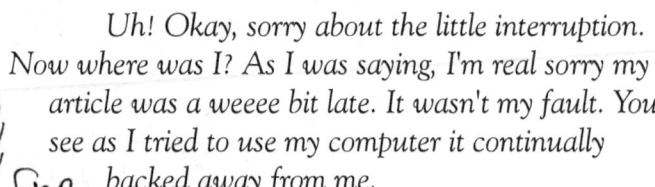

Uh! Okay, sorry about the little interruption. Now where was I? As I was saying, I'm real sorry my article was a weeee bit late. It wasn't my fault. You see as I tried to use my computer it continually backed away from me.

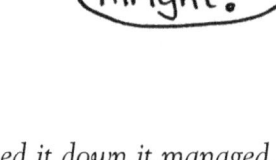

No matter how I strapped it down it managed to get away from me, and------ Okay, okay! I confess, I confess! It was I who couldn't get my act together this time.

Confession is great for the soul, isn't it? Besides, my article was the first one in Charlotte's hand, last issue; so now I feel much better.

I recently returned from a 9-day trip to West Palm (Juno Beach), Florida. I attended 7 days of certification training, for nutritional counseling. The trip, as a whole, was both tedious and enjoyable. We were in class all day on the fourth. Our instructor fed us a homemade breakfast each morning and lunch almost every day.

On the fourth after the fireworks, she took us for a midnight walk on the beach because the moon was full. Things were going well until someone got the bright idea of going for a swim. I told them to go right ahead because I never get in anything deeper than my bath tub, and as far as that big beautiful, but monster-like ocean, I only sit and watch it. Well, you won't believe this, but I let them talk me into going in, but I made them promise to hold onto me. What a sight it was with 3 ladies hanging onto me with my teeth chattering as we stepped into the ocean.

They pulled me further and further away from the shore as I screeched, "I'VE GOT 7 GRANDBABIES. I'M NOT READY TO DIE!!" The waves were enormous and every time one came towards us, which was every few seconds, my eyes grew bigger and I screeched louder. As each wave hit they yelled to me to relax and let it lift me up and carry me. Thank God they were rolling in towards the shore. Believe me, it must have been quite a spectacle for the few moon watchers that were out. After a while I quieted down and tried to enjoy it as much as possible, but I was too ready to get my feet back on dry land. You should have seen me scrambling out of that water.

SPEAKING OF GRANDCHILDREN

I learned that the gift package I sent Raven, my youngest, didn't go over very well. It was an assortment of chewable supplements: Multi-vitamins, calcium, Elderberry for the immune system, antioxidants, etc. They were pleasant tasting and the same goodies the other grandbabies received and enjoyed. Anita said that Raven wouldn't take any of them; she gave quite a performance whenever the subject came up. "Why do I need to take this stuff? It's horrible, and I'm going to throw up!" She really laid it on thick.

Raven is 8 years old now, going on 59, and has been accepted in an advanced academic school. She is in the Gifted Class of the school she currently attends. When she was 5 or so and her little friends came over to play, she would try to teach them games that were over their heads. She would keep switching to a new game, looking for one they could understand. Then she would get frustrated and says things like "well, I guess we can't play this one!" She has quite a personality.

LUCY LOCKET
FEBRUARY 2002

Thanks Charlotte for mailing me a copy of the last newsletter. You are perfectly right about making a habit of putting my copy in the book, even if I don't have the time to punch holes and do it properly. Believe it or not, that's what I normally do, but something must have distracted me. Also, you admonished everyone to slow down and RELAX; Actually, I think that is a very

'GRAND IDEA'. Matter of fact, I think I will look into it a bit more seriously.

That tornado Barbara told us about last issue brought back old memories of when I worked at General Telephone Electronic Data Services 1974 - 1981. My office was on the top floor and was mostly glass. I'll never forget my fear of those dreaded daily funnel clouds.

I would be sitting at my desk watching the sky grow dark right before my eyes, and I would say, "OH, MY GOD, here we go again!" I could never decide whether to grab my favorite plant and my purse, then make a mad dash for 1rst floor or crawl under my desk. What I ultimately did was to sit there frozen, staring out at the storm, having my pencils for a snack. All kidding aside, I really had a serious problem with rainstorms in those days. What happened? Did you gals lock me outside in fowl weather or something, when I was little? Go ahead, and fess up all of you, I forgive you.

TWERP'S Corner:
NOVEMBER 2002

I drove Joey to Atlanta, to get the remainder of his belongings that he left there while he was at school. I asked Tom to take care of my plants while I was gone, and feed the fish.

There was a huge Calla Lily plant I had just received; it was sitting right by the fish tank. When I got home I was horrified to see my plant totally wilted to the floor. All the leaves were literally drooped and ugly.

I wanted to cry. Tom walked right by it every morning to feed the fish and didn't even notice it. When I called him into the room to ask him about the plant, he said, "What's wrong with it? Isn't that pitiful? If I go somewhere again I'll have to get a plant sitter. (smile)

TWERP'S Corner
NOVEMBER 2002

I'm learning to be a gardener. I've always been used to indoor plants. I have never really cared for flowers because they die so quickly. But it's fun simply getting my hands in the dirt, indoors or out. While working in the garden, there is the most beautiful large, fat, white and yellow cat that loves to soak on our back deck. She's absolutely gorgeous! I love cats but I'm allergic to them. So I've found that I have to keep my distance. I have petted the alley cats in our old neighborhood now and then, and I did ok as long as I wasn't around them too long. But I eyed this particular beautiful creature all the time.

One day as I happily went out to the mailbox, to get my mail, "Beauty" as I call her, was on my front porch and started to run as I opened the door. I called and wooed her until she slowly crept up to me. I started petting her. She turned over and let me stroke her stomach. This kept up for only a minute or two. I went out to the mailbox, and by the time I got back in the house, my right eye had started itching. Then it started swelling in the corner.

I splashed cold water on it, hoping it would comfort my eye a little, but it only got worse.

I decided I'd better take an allergy pill. I did, but my eye kept on swelling. It was unreal! I looked in the mirror and saw a monster staring back at me. The film on the white of my eye was filled with fluid where it bulged out over my lower eyelid.

I kid you not! In all my years of allergy suffering, I have never seen anything like it on myself or anyone else. It was uncanny; It hurt so bad! I could hardly close my eye because of the gigantic bubble.

My eye stayed that way all day and all night. The next morning my eye was still sore and slightly swollen. It didn't get back to normal for 2 or 3 days. I vowed then and there never to touch that demonic cat again. That had to be the devil in a cat's body! Seriously, I didn't know how I would handle her in the future. I wanted to stay as far from her as I could.

One day I was outside, and Up walks "Demon".... I mean, "Beauty." I froze in my tracks. She sauntered towards me meowing softly. My mind started racing, "Devil or cat.... cat or devil?" "What to do?".... "SCAT! GET OUT OF HERE!! GET!!!" I heard come out of my mouth. The cat ran one way and I ran the other. I guess I totally confused her. Whenever she sees me she steers clear of me. I guess she says, "There's that ding-a-ling!" So much for cats.

LUCY LOCKET'S Corner
NOVEMBER 2002

We are still talking about the family reunion. I only just got our film developed and enjoyed sharing them with everyone that didn't join us. It was a pleasurable, as well as, a fun time seeing family that I didn't recognize because it has been so long. Kenny, of course, hasn't changed at all. He still looks like Daddy and is doing the same thing he was doing when I last saw him ---- singing his heartout! Wasn't he great?

The funniest thing that happened was, when I was around Barbara, I kept noticing that a very hefty, tall male was always several steps behind her. For a while I just thought Barbara had suddenly gotten rich and her bodyguard was watching over her.

I was somewhat intimidated by his size so it took me a while to ask her, "Barbara, who is that big guy who keeps following you around?" She said,"that's your nephew, Ronnie." It was so good seeing how the Lord healed him after He worked all the other miracles in Ronnie's life. We really do have some wonderful testimonies in our family. Between the two of us, Ronnie and I could almost write a book.

Jessie, I have done something drastic, I started taking piano lessons with Pam, our music director at church.

I became frustrated when I completely forgot how to play that beautiful song I let you hear over the phone. I went through a period of time when I couldn't practice and LO! And BEHOLD! When I sat down to play, I couldn't remember one chord.

I was disappointed because of the time and effort I had put into making up and adding fancy stuff to a simple piece of sheet music. I thought, "that's it, I am going to begin taking lessons and learn how to read the notes properly." Pam told me she would not consider teaching me, unless I made the commitment to practice every day. So, I "Bit The Bullet." You ought to see me racing down the stairs to get in a 30-minute practice. I thought I was through with my chores for the night and could finally go to bed. It is strange having to go all the way back to the basics to learn the essentials. Teresa and Lisa always remind me of how you taught yourself piano all of these years, and how you never gave up. Well, Sister Girl, I'm going to be just like you.

TWERP'S Corner
JUNE 2003

I'm finally going to be an honest-to-goodness outside gardener. I love it now. I had to pour over umpteen 'How To' books on plants and flowers. Tom has been taking care of the mowing. He kept trying to get me on the riding mower. But I knew if I did that, then it would become my permanent job. No thanks! I have enough irons in the fire. Well, one day we were trying to beat the rain and the grass was overdue for cutting. He asked me if I would mow while he trimmed with the weed cutter. Reluctantly I said ok. I had never even sat on the thing. He showed me how to start it and gave me detailed instructions. Ok, it seemed easy enough. After all it was just like driving a car... why, I've been driving over half of my life. Right? How complex could this be?

I started the motor... ok. Put it in gear... ok. Put down the blade... very good. Off I went, putt-putt... about 2 miles an hour. Say, this was not so bad. I maneuvered that mower up and down, back and forth, being careful of the hills and steering clear of the drop offs. Tom would stop now and then and just look at me. He must have looked at the size of our lawn, 3 sides equal the size of a small park, then looked at the cloudy sky, and me cruising at my

ridiculous speed and thought, "This will never do!" Just as I was passing him, he reached out and turned up the speed. Off I flew, my mouth and eyes wide open, legs flailing, zigzagging like a drunk driver... at 5 mph. It seemed like 50 mph. I felt like I was on the 500 raceway! (smile)

So long, for now, family. I love you all!

                    Love Always,
                    Jessie Mae

Those Holland Kids

LUCY LOCKET'S CORNER
JUNE 2003

It looks like we are in the midst of my favorite time of year, TORNADO SEASON. I'm not terrified of the threats and warnings like I used to be back in Indiana. I came home from exercising at Stone Mountain, one day, only to hear storm alert sirens on the television.

We were ordered to take cover immediately. The only place in my house away from any windows is in a lower level hall entrance. So there I was on the floor between many pillows with my feet propped up, peacefully involved in my reading, waiting for the high winds to come; it never did. You see, I kept the door cracked a little for a clear view of the window in the next room.

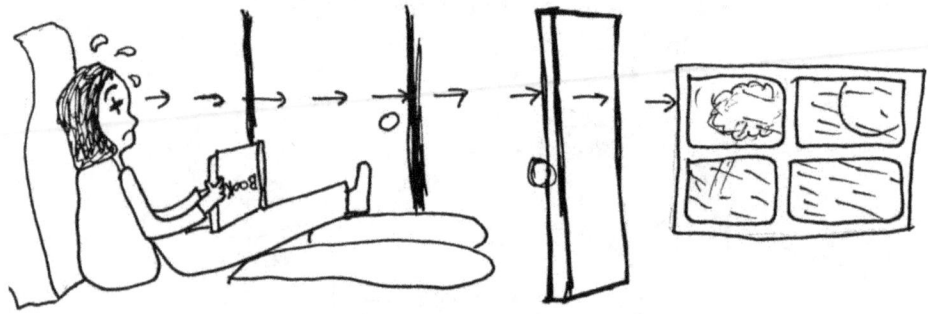

The next morning, I heard that it hit the Northlake area, which is ONLY A FEW MILES to the west of my house. There, the hail beat up cars, etc. pretty good and the storm TRAVELLED and PASSED RIGHT in FRONT of my area by less than a mile and did some major damage up the road. Then it went on its merry way. I had only seen a few drops of hail and not much wind at all. I thought to myself, "I can deal with this". The scripture of Psalms 91 came to my mind: A thousand may fall at my side, 10 thousand at my right hand but it shall not come nigh or near me."

Jessie, I'm really hanging in there with the piano lessons. I'm determined to be just like you. I'm now ready to recite 'Silver Bells' for you. I honestly couldn't do it when you asked me. Pam, my teacher, first assigned me the music in November and it was like a mountain that I couldn't get over. Jessie, it was so funny how I was having such a problem with it. Playing by ear and by memory all those years really makes learning to read notes as written a true challenge. I could tell she was surprised that, I was wrestling so much with that silly little song. Finally Pam said, "Well, I guess we'll just have to keep working at it and you'll have it right by next year. We can be certain you'll have at least one holiday song under your belt by next Christmas". I wanted to forget Silver Bells forever (smile), but 'Pammie' wouldn't give up. I was pouting inside, even though I appreciated her sincerity.

Jessie, How is life without Iggy and life in your new home? I KNOW YOU HAVE A CAT ISSUE,,,,,,SO,,,,,,,,,, What do you suppose I shall do with my 2 new precious critters when you come for our reunion? We really need to talk about this. Of course, my kittens will be so healthy and clean, I can't imagine you having a problem with them because of allergies. Also, there is an air purification system on my furnace, which is supposed to eliminate cat dander, among many other things. So, honey, my cats will be so clean you'll have them stirring your soup for you with their paws.

BIBBA'S CORNER
FEBRUARY 2004

Now, for the episode in Indianapolis. Charlotte and Jessie, you both know how paranoid we are around our sister Donna the "Health Guru". We are almost afraid to go to a restaurant with her. It's always, "You know you shouldn't eat this or that". For instance, after we left the health clinic in Greenwood Ind., we decided to have lunch at the Panera Bread restaurant in the shopping mall. (They have delicious bread). We got our plates with salad, bread and etc. and sat down. Donna looked at our plates and the scolding began. Finally, Donna had to leave the room, for something or the other. I thought I would pass out LAUGHING. it was so funny, watching Charlotte gulping down that bread, while Donna was away from the table.

LUCY LOCKET'S Corner
FEBRUARY 2004

It was good seeing all of you at our family reunion planning committee meeting in October. I thoroughly enjoyed hanging out at Jessie's lovely new home; I look forward to coming back again, after she has recuperated from our wild

visit. When I do, I'm going to kick off my shoes and head straight for her patio and deck, plop down with a good book and let the sun pamper me all day.

February 2004

Charlotte, you and I have been doing quite a bit of conversing, since the last newsletter, concerning the family reunion and some other things. I remember how (when you worked for that bakery) you were often frustrated, when greedy customers ate up all of your cookie samples. Then they had the audacity to ask you to put out some more and stand right there, like hungry wolves, watching you take the wrapping paper off. But, I must say, that it's good that your cookie cart is not in the places that I shop or you would see me peering into your sample tray, right along with the starving wolves. Since I don't buy, bake or keep sweets in my house, I always enjoy having one bite of something every now and then. So I am an occasional sampler who has no intention of purchasing anything. But I do, at least, wait until you take the wrapper off and set it up or I'll come back later. You may even find me walking a few circles around your counter, pretending not to be interested, while keeping one eye on your not-quite-ready, samples.

Then I will have one or two bites and will not be interested in sweets any more. I guess that's one way that I keep it out of my house and out of my system, the majority of the time.

The week after Christmas was very nice here in Atlanta. The weather turned very mild and spring like, in the mid 60's. We certainly could have used the pleasant skies on the days before Christmas to make small errands less complicated. I set out to make a simple and quick trip to the supermarket to pick up the items from a well thought out list. I was driving Teresa's 'MONSTER' Dodge Ram truck. My errand that started out as a simple one-hour trip, suddenly turned into a disastrous but hilarious adventure. When I left home it was very cold but not rainy. I entered the market whistling and merry. Lo! and Behold! When I rolled my cart outside, it was pouring rain. I said "Oh well, I'll just flip open my umbrella and everything -- Shall Be Well --." So off I went across the parking lot with my oversized umbrella and my too heavy basket of groceries. It happened to be uphill to the truck and my cart was getting heavier and more difficult to control with one hand while holding the umbrella with the other. By the time I finally made it to the truck, I was almost out of breath and a little frustrated by the untimely rain. I struggled to open the ridiculously heavy and over-sized door of the truck, that usually knocks me over on a good day. I finally decided that it was definitely going to take both my hands on this day. When I let go of the cart to open the door, the cart took off rolling back down the parking lot. So I would leave the door and chase after the cart and bring it back.

After several frantic sprints down the hill with umbrella in hand, I ultimately managed to get the monster door and the wild runaway cart to stand still at the same time. I finished loading the groceries in the truck and headed for one last quick stop. I had put some bags on the passenger seat and was confident that they were secure enough for the short trip home. When I arrived at my unplanned stop before home, it was more convenient to take out what I needed from the passenger side, -- So I Thought --. As I opened the door, the apples and sweet potatoes rolled off the seat and down onto the pavement. I tried desperately to grab them before they began rolling but because my oversized umbrella kept getting hung up on the open door of the truck cab, I managed to only retrieve the

sweet potatoes.

I finally made the wise decision to abandon my protective shield from the cold rain, which up to now hadn't been very effective, and turn my energies toward saving my Christmas dinner. It was too late; two of the apples had picked up unusual momentum, on the rain- drenched concrete parking lot, and jeered back at me as I chased after them.

Back at home, too many hours later, I was too relieved to be rid of the monster truck (which, by now, had sprouted horns), the wild & unruly grocery cart, and the mischievous apples, (which, by the way, I never caught). The entire eventful errand really caused me to laugh at myself and see the comical side of my life.

FEBRUARY 2004

Lately I began thinking about bowling and remembering how Cecelia and I used to spend a lot of time at the bowling allies playing game after game. We were young, energetic and strong. Cecelia used a sixteen-pound ball and would sling it down the alley as though it weighed 10 pounds. Most women like me used an eleven or twelve pound ball. We were very good and knew exactly where to lay that ball down. It was nothing new for us to bowl a 200 Plus game. We would stay at the lanes until wee hours of the morning. I decided to take up bowling again and went prepared to play 6 or 7 games, only to discover that the price per game has skyrocketed to $4.00. I quickly changed my mind about hanging out there all evening. I was also surprised to find that I had not completely lost my touch; my highest score was 176.

Every time I made a strike I stayed out on the lane for a few seconds and did my famous Billy 'White Shoes' Johnson dance, to taunt my competition. I've gone back to the lanes several times since, and believe I'll stick with it.

BIBBA'S CORNER
OCTOBER 2004

A few weeks ago, I was awakened by the sound of a car motor running. Our

Those Holland Kids

bedroom faces the front. I got up and looked out the window and saw a car parked in front by the mailbox post that we share with two other neighbors. I watched for awhile, but nobody got out of the car. After about 10-15 minutes, I called the neighbors across the street. I knew they hadn't gone to bed because their lights were still on. The car was still parked with the motor running and the headlights on. I told our neighbor what was going on, and asked if any of his kids were there and parked their car on the street instead of in their driveway. He said there was no one at his house. By the way it was around 11:30 p.m. when all this was going on. Our neighbor thought it was suspicious. At that point, I awakened George and told him my concerns. He agreed with me, so I said, "Call the police". He said, "No, you call them." You can guess what I told him in so many words, in a nice way of course. All the time, the devil was having a field day with me.

When I checked again, I saw the person get out of the car and started messing with the mailboxes. I still could not tell who it was, and that's when I almost freaked out. That Did It! I immediately called 911! The 911 operator asked me what was the problem. After I relayed to her what was happening, she must have thought it was a valid complaint because she said they would send someone right out. I asked her not to have them use the siren so she said they wouldn't use it. Meanwhile, the car left before the police arrived. They sent two patrol cars,

thinking it was something BIG. They met me at the door and asked me to describe the incident, person and the car. I felt so stupid after I said that. As for the man, he looked like he may have been a Caucasian, I wasn't sure. The officer said "did you look in the mailbox'? I said, "no, I wasn't about to go out there," So he finally went out and looked into all three mailboxes. Now here is the rest of the story as Paul Harvey says ----

The officer found a piece of paper in my mailbox. When I looked at the paper, it was a church information flyer that our pastor put in there. I was so upset with my pastor,,, I really could have smacked him if he was in front of me. No, I wouldn't, of course, but I felt like it. Afterwards I had to laugh. I have known our pastor, Warren Jr. since he was a teenager. I feel like a second mother to him. He could have, at least, let us know what he was going to do. The next day I confronted him and asked why he sat in front of the house for such a long time. He said he was reading something. Also he said he knows that we go to bed early and didn't want to disturb us. After I told him what I went through, he just about passed out laughing. I'll admit it was funny, when I finally cooled off.

That's all for now,
Barb

SHARKEY'S Corner
OCTOBER 2004

At this time in October, I am writing my letter while in Warsaw, Indiana. Barbara and I are here attending the final Winsome Women's Retreat. We sisters and (even Mom, a couple times), had been attending these Retreats, since back in the 70's. We got away from coming in the 80's or early 90's. It is so good being here again, and seeing the women who started this ministry. They are much older looking now (aren't we all?), and some are not here any longer. The speakers are women from way back, also --- now older and more seasoned. They are so interesting to watch, as well as listen to.

When we first came here, Barbara was complaining about ---- how tired she was. "I just have to get some rest." "I have to get some sleep," she moaned. Well, Saturday night, when we were ready for bed --- I was glad that we were going to get some sleep earlier than Friday night ---- I, also, was tired.

But, Sis was commenting on news that was on TV. She commented ---- and she expounded --- she made exclamations ---- and commented some more. All the while, I was lying in my bed ---- fighting to keep my eyes open ---- and saying ---- "uh, uh" ---- every now and then ---- wondering ---- "what's with Barb?" --- -- "who gave her a talking pill?" ---- "I thought she was so tired! ---- "when is she going to sleep?" After awhile, Barb cried out --- "Oh, my God, it's 11 o'clock! ---- How did I stay up this late?!"

TWERP'S Corner
OCTOBER 2004

I've been busy with my piano students and enjoying them so much. Although at times
my patience has been sorely challenged. At first all my students were sweet little girls. Then, lo and behold, I started getting little boys. Not just little boys, but HYPER ones. Lord, Help Me! One Special One…. and I can say now, he truly is special. It came with much prayer and faith in God. I kid you not!!!

His name is Jonah; he came to me last Sept. --A nine-year-old whirlwind--. The first day his mom brought him to my home, he came in the door and fell flat out on my hallway floor. I looked at him wide-eyed. His mom, used to his antics, just stood there with her arms folded and just looked at him. Since it was evident that nothing was going to change, I said, "Ok Jonah, let's get to the lesson." He lay there. My mind went haywire, "Lord, What have I gotten myself

into?" Finally, his mom spoke up with authority and told him to get up. Reluctantly, he got up.

That was just the beginning of my trial. He's the type that thinks he knows more than the teacher. He doesn't believe in doing his best, just as long as he does it, no matter how sloppy. That drives me up the wall. When I tell him to repeat the exercise, he folds his arm, drops his head and whines, "Why?" then proceeds to pout. Through clinched teeth, I respond, "Because I asked you to."

This went on for a couple of weeks, till I got ready to tell his mom to stop wasting her money and bring him back, after he has grown up some. It seemed like he just was not able to grasp learning. And I had gotten to the place where I was actually getting the sweats, as I watched the clock, knowing he would be here soon.

His mom had told me that he was borderline A.D.D. Even though my heart went out to her I had to think of myself. My golden years are supposed to be Golden, right? Anyway, after a session of tension (on my part) and pouting, arm folding, and total rebellion...no, (not on my part)...(but it very well could have been) my mind was made up to tell his mom. But for some reason the words would not come out. That night the Lord laid on my heart to pray for the little guy. Now isn't that some-thing, me a woman of faith didn't even THINK to PRAY. Pray I did, and I truly believed that God was going to intervene. And true to His Nature, God came to my rescue, as well as Jonah's and his mom's.

I saw the difference that following week. I almost fell off the bench when I saw the sudden transformation. I knew God was going to work, but I didn't think it would be that soon. He started catching on right away. I was so pleased. Praise the Lord! There was hope for the child. Today, he is just blowing our minds. He sped through Book One and is now finishing up Book Two. He has an awesome memory. I teach the students songs that I write out and they can memorize. He learns them in one or two weeks.

Now don't get me wrong, there has been a truly dramatic change in Little Jonah. But he doesn't have his Halo yet. I guess the Lord is letting me know that I'll always need Him. When Jonah comes over it never fails that he rings the

doorbell and hides behind the shrubs as if I don't know it's him. When I FINALLY get him in the house, it's time for me to get braced. He is the only student who is not intimidated by the piano keys. He literally bangs! At first, I try not to say anything thinking it will soon pass. When it doesn't, I told him to try not to bang on the keys. He lightens up for a minute, then it's back to business as usual. Finally I say, "You're hurting my ears!" He has the nerve to say,
"Then stop them up!" ----"Ok, Lord, I need your Grace to help me NOT to do something unkind to this child!

Now, I am so proud of this young boy. I see why God had me stick in there with him. The boy is going to be good; he has great potential. He will be going into Book 3 next week. I do a lot of review. Even though he doesn't like it, he no longer complains. His mom is as pleased as I am. She also has been praying for him and working with him about his attitude. God is Good!!!

I not only have young people but also adults. One student I had was LaDonna. Some of you met her when she catered our food for our Reunion Committee Meeting here at my home.

I don't know if anyone noticed her fingernails. They were, about 2 inches long. They actually curved at the end. She has had these long

nails for years and they never hamper her in whatever she needs to get done. It's amazing just to watch her do anything. Well, one day she decided she wanted to learn to play
the piano. O..o..o..kay!!! And learn she did.

The only drawback was listening to those claws click-clacking on the piano keys. Oh, Lord!!! She was so happy, grinning from ear to ear and clack, clack, clacking away.

One day, when I went for her lesson, I was shocked to see that she had cut her nails. Even though they were still about 1 inch long, to think she would actually part with them to play piano was awesome.

TWERP'S continued

Donna, when you spoke about Jenny bowling, I remember her chewing gum, that beautiful long hair flying, and her slinging that heavy ball down the alley with lightning speed at those poor helpless pins. Every time she got up to bowl I can just imagine those pins sweating and wishing they could run.

chapter 12

September 2007
Those Holland Kids, "now"

The late afternoon traffic on Interstate 65N is unusually congested. The white four-door Honda blends in to the flow from Nashville to Indianapolis. Donna has driven this route many times from Atlanta. It is always therapeutic, a great way to relax.

"There's the highway sign I love to see; 51 miles to Indianapolis," she says aloud to break the silence in the car. She had been thinking about how her life has changed since her health has greatly improved. Since those unsettled years of her long illness, she has purchased and redecorated the home she now enjoys. Even though she has not reentered the corporate job environment she stays busy with her nutritional counseling.

"My visits home always seem to be just what the doctor ordered so to speak; two weeks away from Atlanta is a wonderful prescription and always lifts my spirits. The thing that's not good, though, is being away from my church and uninvolved in ministry activities.

"There's my exit to Charlotte's coming up—"

****

Barbara has just finished her usual daily chores; giving George his medicines, preparing the meal, and tidying up the kitchen. "Thank God," she is thinking. "My quiet time with the Lord and in His word this morning is helping me get through this day. I still have a few things to do before Donna comes. Our sister-reunions have been transformed into individual visits at various times. Since George's first heart attack he can't be left alone so my travels have become few."

Having things caught up to the moment, Barbara stops to relax for a few minutes. "God is truly good. Even way up into my seventies I'm still hanging in there health-wise with no major problems. As for this old house, it's been a real challenge; even so, it's comfortable, it's mine, and it's just around the corner from Cecelia's old house. And it's a blessing that I've found time to make a few upgrades.

"I also have to keep up my stamina for the work I do at the church, the bookkeeping, etc. I still have to go over and check on Linda at the assisted living facility. When Donna comes we'll go over together. Linda has come a long way since she suffered that stroke a few years ago. She was fifty percent paralyzed, but now she is able to talk and can get around on her walker.

"Well, I need to get up and get moving. I guess my break is over—"

****

Jessie turns the key locking the door of the large youth center at her church. She gives the door a quick nudge to make certain it is secure. Turning to walk to her car, she slows her pace to assess the finished product of Tom's skilled construction work. The youth center with its large gymnasium stands beside the sanctuary on the corner lot of a busy intersection. The parking lot stretches the entire length of both structures.

"It's been twenty-five years," Jessie sighs, "years of pleasure, heart-aches, and struggles, spiritual growth, joy, and bonding with God's lovely children." Unlocking her car, she remembers that the next few days will be both hectic and anticipatory. "Doctors appointments are always challenging for both Tom and me. And then there is our Pastor's Silver Anniversary Celebration this weekend. And, of course, Donna is coming."

Jessie pulls her car into her driveway and moves slowly up the walkway to the front door. Every step still requires effort. Last year's heart surgery has left her somewhat weak. Only recently she has learned that she was born with a hole in her heart and her left and right ventricles are reversed. Tom is also in recovery mode from surgery due to a brain tumor.

Jessie notices she is experiencing some mixed emotions. "Even though the pastor's celebration and Donna's visit are both enjoyable occasions they still require extra strength that I just don't seem to have. Nevertheless, I know all things work together for the good of those who love the Lord and are called by His name—"

****

Marcia parks her brand new car and heads for the kitchen to make dinner preparations. Only yesterday she returned from a wonderful trip—five fantastic days in New York—a gift from one of her daughters. Several months ago, she was blessed with a vacation in the Bahamas and last year it was Hawaii. So Marcia is satisfied to be spending this time at home. "Oh, don't get me wrong," she is thinking apologetically, "I absolutely love traveling and seeing places I never thought I'd ever witness. It's just that with Donna on the way and Jessie and Tom's pastoral function coming up I have a lot to look forward to right here."

Maneuvering with efficiency around her kitchen Marcia begins thinking about the last several years. It seems ages ago when she developed gangrene in her foot and reluctantly agreed to amputation. She ponders the painful ordeal. "I am so very surprised and thankful for the way I have been able to adjust to life with an artificial limb. I have learned that 'God is Great' all the time.

"Speaking of our great and wonderful Lord, I just remembered my dear brother Kenny said he would call me today. Since the newsletters inspired him to participate we've been hearing from him often. For many years, before and after Mom died, he pretty much separated himself from us all. I'm sure it must have been tough being one of only two guys in the midst of seven gals." Marcia smiles at the thought.

"It would be nice if my next surprise vacation gift is a trip to Arizona to visit Kenny and his family. I'd have the chance once more to hear him crooning like Johnny Mathis at the Karaoke Bar (chuckle, chuckle)—"

****

"Jim, please hurry up with the vacuuming," Charlotte pleads. "Donna said she was only fifteen minutes away." Charlotte tries her best not to seem ungrateful that Jim is at least trying to help. She has actually succeeded amazingly well at shifting gears from a life of being strictly a working housewife to one of managing all the home repairs and household finances.

Charlotte thinks back on Jim's several bouts of congestive heart failure. They left him unable to do any of the host of things he used to manage with great expertise. "After thirty-five years of leaving it all up to him I guess I really have graciously mastered every aspect of maintaining a home and all of its finances. During the time when Jim was not expected to live and was in a coma I remember having not the slightest idea about the details of even how he had recently purchased our brand new car. What a transformation of mind!

"Oh, my goodness, I've missed Jim's four o'clock medications again!" Charlotte drops the stack of laundry on the bed and heads for the kitchen trying desperately to concentrate on getting the pills dispersed correctly. Even so, her mind travels back to her four-legged babies. "They were my pride and joy. Now they've all gone on to 'Doggie Heaven' one at a time from old age, etc. I really miss them. Thank God for Jessie! She blessed me with an oil canvas portrait of each of them.

"Jim, come on and take your meds," Charlotte calls, anxious to put the wraps on everything. "I think when Donna gets here we'll call Leonard. He left a message earlier. She'll definitely want to talk to him. Life is full of surprises; we pray for miracles and when they come we're shocked." Charlotte smiles, "Leonard still lives in California though he's been divorced for a very long time. For twenty-plus years he was totally missing from our lives. Then last year he surprised and blessed each of us with a Merry Christmas phone call."

Charlotte continues, "There is one thing Leonard did, for which I will always be grateful. He helped lead Ritchie to receive the Baptism in the Holy Spirit. Of course, Ritchie still struggled for many years, up and down, in and out. Most of that time, he lived on the streets. Finally he accepted my constant urging to get help. He contacted The Dream Center, a Christian rehabilitation facility, and became a resident. Three years later he came home a different individual, a new creature in Christ Jesus. He now lives in Atlanta and is married to Gayle, a sweet, beautiful Christian woman. They are involved in outreach ministries and are very dedicated to their church. The Lord God truly answered this Holland mother's prayers for her son to live a normal life with an address, a home, and a family.

Charlotte begins to dwell on her work over the years with the family newsletters. "I believe the greatest work and blessing of The Lord is how

He has used our family newsletters over the years to reach out to Daddy's sisters, brothers, nieces, and nephews. As children, we were not close to them; we rarely spent quality time with each other. So I know for a fact that they have learned more about us through our newsletter articles than they could have ever dreamed possible.

"My heart is warmed even now when I think of how our newsletters opened the door to wonderful family reunions with Daddy's people. We now enjoy these family reunions every other year. The first Holland Family Reunion was held in Detroit and the second was here in Indianapolis. The food was delicious and everyone had a joyous time.

"The decorating committee, Donna, Anita, and Suzanne did a splendid job! And just to think that prior to the first reunion Donna had never even met Daddy's side of the family. So to picture her working with Anita and Suzanne (Daddy's nieces) hanging balloons and streamers all over the banquet room is an awesome visual.

"The more I mull over how far we have come from a time when none of us had even heard from our baby bro, Kenny, I get goose bumps. He finally joined us with articles for the newsletters and is a part of our family reunions. He even took over the turn-table furnishing us with beautiful music to dine by. And in between his disc jockeying he serenaded us with his Johnny Mathis-like renditions.

"Anita graced us as Mistress of Ceremonies for the entire evening program, hosting The Holland Revue Talent Show. Donna conducted a group game between performances, a game of winning prizes and losing prizes. It was extremely hilarious and a lot of fun. Donna surprised everyone with her wit as she added little quips and stories along the way. I always knew she was a talker, being a seminar speaker. But this was a new side of her that everyone enjoyed. And, oh, what talent we have in our overall family! The singers, dancers, and piano players were out of sight!

"The talent show extended very late into the evening and I was surprised to see who hung right in there with the young people. Aunt Jessie and Aunt Sarah (Daddy's sisters) were as bright-eyed and bushy-tailed as when the day first began. I was so pleased and thankful for the presence of these two beautiful and strong women. We were so proud of our reunion president, Ernie (Daddy's nephew). We presented him an elegant gift; a pen engraved with 'Ernest Holland, the 1rst Holland C.E.O.'"

Charlotte glances outside through the sunroom windows to see if by chance Donna happens to be driving into the subdivision—

****

The white four-door Honda glistens in the setting sun as Donna makes the careful turn into Charlotte's subdivision. The enormous waterfall on the left that marks the entrance to the subdivision makes its usual visual statement. "That waterfall feature must make a great drawing card to the closing table," Donna muses. "It's breathtaking!" She is quite familiar with the landscape from her previous visits.

"I'm happy for Charlotte. She had wanted to move out of her old house for quite a while into a maintenance-free environment. If they hadn't done that I don't know how she could have managed her many crucial obligations. I have to say she made an awesome choice. Her individual unit actually faces the waterfall."

Donna continues driving purposely slowly toward the single-story gray brick and stone structure. She follows the perfectly manicured shrubbery around to the side of the house and garage. "This is certainly de je vu! How many times have I done this?" She pulls into her usual spot beside the garage. She pauses only to collect her purse and carry-all bag but by the time she reaches the garage door it opens.

"I saw you driving in, Sis." Charlotte walks briskly toward her, arms outstretched—

EPILOGUE

We sincerely thank you for choosing this book. It was not by chance that you did so. God had a purpose in this documentation being put together; to show the world how an average family can pray together and trust God through good times and bad.

Those Holland Kids started out with a bang writing their newsletter issues. At that time they felt young at heart, soul, and body. But as the years rolled past many roadblocks appeared. Family health issues and loss of stamina from aging brought our writings first to a slowing down then to a screeching halt. However, the die had already been cast. Despite the attacks from our enemy, the devil, many prayers were answered; one being that my son Ritchie came out from a life on the streets of Los Angeles and is now married and active in ministry.

The newsletters formed a deep bond that could not be broken. We now keep in touch often by phone, e-mail, and visits. Hopefully this book will be an inspiration to families who have difficulty getting and staying close to each other. We have attempted to relay the years that we shared together, as a family. We realize our bonding experiences may not be unique for many families, especially during the depression. But as times have changed and the technological age has escalated, the family structure has begun to crumble. We have certainly had our share of problems; but God is faithful and has always helped us through them all. We praise God for His goodness and His mercy.

God's heart is for families; always has been and always will be. Our proof is Acts 16:31, "Believe in the Lord Jesus Christ (give yourself up to Him, take yourself out of your own keeping and entrust yourself into His keeping) and you will be saved (and this applies both to) you and your household, as well." I truly believe the Lord will use each reader as an instrument for His will. Time is short! "Now unto Him who is able to (carry out His purpose and) do super-abundantly, far over and above all that we (dare) ask or think (infinitely beyond our highest prayers, desires, thoughts, hopes, or dreams), according to the power that worketh in us" (Ephesians 3:20).

God Bless You!

Holland Family Memories

Those Holland Kid's Parents
the late Kenneth and Idona

To The Family

I must leave you for a little while:
  Please do not grieve and shed wild tears,
  And hug your sorrow to you through the years.

But start out bravely with a gallant smile;
  And for my sake and in my name,
  Live on and do all things the same.

Feed not your loneliness on empty days,
  But fill each waking hour in useful ways

Feed not your loneliness on empty days,
  But fill each waking hour in useful ways.

Reach out your hand in comfort and in cheer,
  And I in turn will comfort you and hold you near.

And never, never be afraid to die,
  For I am waiting for you in the sky.

One of Those Holland Kids the late Cecelia (Jenny)

From left: Those Holland Kids - Marcia, Barbara, Charlotte, Donna and Jessie - at a women's conference

From left: Twin Leonard, Donna and Kenny finally get together at a family reunion after 30 years - and Twin Linda

Endorsements

The Book, "Those Holland Kids" then and now, creates an immense desire to become closer to my siblings and extended family. The book also creates a desire to start a family newsletter. I can attest that Lucy Lockett (Donna – one of the siblings and author) has become a very elegant and creative lady.

Dr. Carolyn Driver
Professor, Beulah Heights University
Atlanta, Georgia

****

This book is easy reading and I highly recommend it. The reader will enjoy the antidotes, humor and serious conversation of the Holland family. This is one of those books that require a hot cup of coffee and a soft relaxing chair to read. Enjoy, and you will find yourself somewhere in its pages.

Suffragan Bishop Larry Hunt, Pastor
Grace Apostolic Church
Indianapolis, Indiana

****

This book demonstrates so clearly the importance of faith in God and continual contact and communication with family, through the good times and bad times. Donna Holland Lawrence has been a blessing in her church by participating in worship music, interpretive dancing, as well as, teaching dance and fundraising.

She has also been integral in teaching and demonstrating a healthy lifestyle, willing to help in any way when asked, and always faithful with tithes and offering. She is such a delight to work with and certainly proves her abilities as an author in this book.

Pastor Mary Simpson
Christ Discipleship Ministries
Fairburn, Georgia

www.ingramcontent.com/pod-product-compliance
Lightning Source LLC
Chambersburg PA
CBHW051752040426
42446CB00007B/337